RISE & FALL
OF THE
NAZIS

RISE & FALL
OF THE
NAZIS

CLAIRE WELCH

Magpie, London

Constable & Robinson Ltd
3 The Lanchesters
162 Fulham Palace Road
London W6 9ER
www.constablerobinson.com

Published by Magpie Books,
an imprint of Constable & Robinson Ltd 2008

Designed by Peran Publishing Services

Thanks to Jeff Durham, Michael Heatley and
Michael Hobbs for their contributions.

A copy of the British Library Cataloguing in
Publication Data is available from the British Library

ISBN-13: 978-1-84529-771-8

Printed and bound in China

1 3 5 7 9 10 8 6 4 2

Contents

Introduction

The Second World War, the mid-twentieth century conflict, was the deadliest, largest war in human history. Fought between the Axis Powers, of which the three largest were Nazi Germany, Fascist Italy and Imperial Japan, and the Allies who comprised Great Britain and the British Empire, France, Poland and eventually other commonwealth countries, Brazil, China and the United States, the war cost the lives of more than 70 million people while more than 100 million military personnel were deployed.

Following a drawn-out, complicated path to the conflict, war finally broke out on Sunday 3 September 1939 when Britain and France declared war on Germany after Adolf Hitler refused to abort his attack on Poland. It would

Adolf Hitler reviews the troops during the victory parade of the 8th Army in Warsaw, Poland, on 5 October 1939.

1

last six years and see some of the most horrendous atrocities committed against mankind ever known, including the Holocaust, the atomic bombings of Hiroshima and Nagasaki, intensive bombings of major cities on both sides, most notably London and Dresden, and major bloody battles in North Africa, the Pacific Ocean, Russia and Europe. A further element of this widespread war, which caused hatred and fear on a scale never seen before, was the experiments that were carried out on innocent people, many children and babies, within the Nazi death camps and in China, where Japan's General Ishii Shiro was responsible for the experiments carried out by Unit 731 in Pingfan.

For most of the previous decade prior to September 1939, both the British Government under then Prime Minister Neville Chamberlain, and the French, led by President Edouard Daladier, had tried to reason and appease Adolf Hitler, who had come to come to power in

German soldiers carry out their anti-aircraft training as Luftwaffe planes fly overhead.

Hitler at the speaker's rostrum during the National Socialist/SA meeting in Dortmund on 9 July 1933.

Nazi Germany in 1933. But, the Austrian-born leader who had relented on his planned invasion of Czechoslovakia was determined. Backed by the Italian Fascist leader Benito Mussolini, who had invaded Ethiopia (then Abyssinia) in 1936, Hitler was to give the Allies no choice. Britain had treaty obligations with Poland, so despite the Depression of the early 1930s, government debt and widespread exhaustion across the country, still recovering from the onslaught of the First World War, Chamberlain led his weary-worn nation into battle.

Other factors fuelled the Second World War after Hitler's planned and expertly executed invasion of Poland. Besides Mussolini's attack on Abyssinia three years earlier, Germany maintained an active partnership with the former Soviet Union (USSR) between August 1939 and June 1941. These two strong nations were to fall out bitterly which eventually would lead to Germany attacking its previous ally. One major difference between

A Junkers JU-88 bomber starts a mission to England.

the Second World War, which affected most of the globe, and other conflicts, particularly the First World War, was the resources available to the opposing sides. These were to change the face of conflict throughout the world forever. New resources included the use of great numbers of tanks and destroyer tank formations, jet aircraft, torpedo bombers, submarines, and, of course, the use of the atomic bomb. It was the first time that an atomic weapon had been used against either military targets or civilians and other newly developed technologies would cost countries, such as the United States, around US$ 1 trillion. This did not include the cost of reconstruction.

Having been bombed by twin-engined bombers and zeppelins during the 1914–1918 conflict, Britain knew on all levels that the Second World War would bring as much danger to the home front as to those fighting on the front. It was another new concept of war to take notice of and while the United Kingdom prepared itself for the inevitable death and destruction that bombers would bring, Germany, now rearmed and working to a new nationalist foreign policy since Hitler's rise to power, made headway with the capture of Denmark and Norway in the spring of 1940. Meanwhile, Japan had been launching full-scale attacks on China since July 1937 with the bombing of Shanghai and Guangzhou. However, it was the bloody massacre in Nanking – known as The Rape of Nanking – in December that year that caused disbelief across the United States and Europe. The fantastical stories that were leaked by eyewitnesses in and around Nanking, although worrying, were, to a certain extent, little regarded by the Allies who were more intent on the activities of Hitler. Sparked by a Chinese bomb in September 1931 which blew

German soldiers cross the Don on a pontoon bridge as they march towards Stalingrad in the summer of 1942.

up a Japanese express train and became known as the "Mukden Incident", the Japanese began to attack China on a regular basis before declaring the outbreak of war between the two nations in July 1937. By the time the

Japanese Imperial Army marched into Nanking five
months later, by now the Chinese capital following the
intense siege at Beijing, they were met by little resistance.
An estimated 300,000 men, women and children were

killed during the six weeks of the Imperial Army's reign of terror, where the streets literally ran with blood, and more than 20,000 women and children, some as young as seven, were raped. Many of these victims were mutilated and killed once they had outlived their usefulness.

By early summer 1940, Germany had captured France and the Low Countries and by June, Italy had declared war and had also attacked France. Britain was next on the agenda for the German army. Hitler quickly realised that as an island, Britain could be cut off from all vital supplies and an attempt was made to do exactly that. First, Hitler needed superiority in the air which he hoped would lead to a full-blown offensive from the sea. He rightly calculated that an attack on Britain would never work from the sea unless the Royal Air Force (RAF) had been, at least, broken or at best, obliterated. His best laid plans never came to fruition, however, and although Germany continued to attack Britain, primarily from the sky, Hitler would never obtain the stronghold on British land he had envisaged. Although Britain had little success on the continent initially there was a degree of victory over the Italian navy in the Mediterranean and a major defeat over Germany when the Battle of Britain (July–October 1940) was won. The battle was the first to be conducted entirely in the air and was the first real test of strategic bombing developed since the First World War. The failure by Hitler's Germany to defeat the RAF or break the spirit of the British Government or its people was considered the Third Reich's first major defeat.

With their partnership in tatters following confrontation, Germany and the Soviet Union found themselves on opposing sides with the latter becoming an integral member of the Allies. In June 1941, Germany invaded the USSR, which proved initially to be highly successful and increased war activities, but German forces found themselves under significant pressure by the winter. Meanwhile, having suffered from increased economic sanctions from the West, including from Britain, the Netherlands and the United States, Japan had withdrawn its troops from mainland China and was trying to negotiate its way out of ever tightening restrictions. But the Japanese were not to be kept back for long and six months after Germany invaded the Soviet Union, Japan was on the offensive with virtually simultaneous attacks against the United States and British assets in Asia. It was December 1941, and by now, Japan had been at war with mainland China for nearly five years. Germany, that same month, then declared war on the United States and the previously separate Asian and European wars

A group of women and girls await execution. Over 2,700 Jews were shot near Liebau in December 1941 during the German occupation of the Baltic states.

compounded into one conflict on a global scale – it was to prove deadly for all nations involved.

Despite the continued headway made by the Axis forces during 1942 the tide was already beginning to turn. On one level it began on the Eastern Front when the Germans backtracked their offensive strikes near the

Caucasus to secure the oil fields. German troops reached Stalingrad where a bitter siege continued for many months resulting in large numbers of casualties on both sides. The east bank of the River Volga became a life-line for the Soviet troops where supplies were brought in at night, while the Sixth Army (the *Wehrmacht*) were eventually

Joseph Goebbels, Minister for Propaganda, calls for *Totaler Krieg* (total war) during his speech in February 1943.

This view of Dresden in 1945 clearly shows the destruction caused by Allied bombers.

surrounded with next to no supplies. It was clear that the Sixth Army would have to surrender by early 1942. They had been surrounded by Soviet forces for more than three months during which time Hitler had ordered that their armour be diverted to the Caucasus. To avoid surrender, the German leader promoted General Friedrich Paulus to Field Marshall. No field marshall had ever surrendered in the history of the German army, but Paulus felt he had no choice and a complete surrender took place on 2 February 1943. It would lead to the collapse of the Sixth Army as a strong fighting force and it was the speech by Joseph Goebbels, the Nazi Propaganda Minister, following these events that would cite this as the turning point for many. Delivered on 18 February 1943 to a carefully selected audience in Berlin, Goebbels made his longest and most famous speech which was intended in part, following the battle of Stalingrad, to rally yet further popularity for the Second World War in light of the fact that the true seriousness of the conflict was becoming evident to all. Goebbels also intended that the speech should convince Aldolf Hitler to give him more power over running the war economy.

Following their own victory at Stalingrad, the Red Army launched a number of offensives over the winter which at first resulted in success over the German forces. But having endured sustained fighting for many months the Red Army were at a disadvantage through tiredness, and their weakened condition saw them lose the territory they had gained to the Germans. Meanwhile, the Allies were gaining ground in Italy and following the invasion of Sicily, Mussolini was fired from office by the King of Italy. The Allies went on to gain a stronghold in mainland Italy on 3 September and on 8 September 1943 the Italians surrendered. The German forces in Italy continued to fight but the Allies captured Rome in June 1944. In Asia, fighting and resistance were just as intense as the Australians and

US forces began a long campaign to reclaim the Solomon Islands, New Britain and New Ireland as well as the Philippines, New Guinea and the Dutch East Indies. In late 1944, the Battle of Leyte Gulf would become one of the largest naval battles in history. Next, the Allies wanted to further isolate the Japanese along the south west Pacific towards Borneo in mid-1945. As well as cutting the Japanese off it gave the Allies the chance to free many prisoners of war (POWs).

Victory was in sight for the Allied forces and on D-Day, 6 June 1944, the Allies invaded Normandy in the north of France which was locked in a stronghold by the Germans.

Liberation of Dachau concentration camp by the US 7th Army on 29 April 1945.

The huge beach assault resulted in a large number of casualties for the Allies during the pre-dawn raid, including British, US and Canadian troops. Following further battles the French Resistance in Paris rallied against German forces on 19 August 1944, and with the help of French forces, liberated the capital city six days later. The German army surrendered. Combined with the Red Army's arrival in Poland in early 1944 which ended the Siege of Leningrad, the Allies began to gain ground. It was December 1944 when German forces made their last major offensive in the West. In February 1945, Winston Churchill, the British Prime Minister, the Soviet leader, Stalin and President of the United States, Franklin D Roosevelt, discussed a post-war Europe at the Yalta Conference. It was to lead to the formation of the United Nations in April that year and the Red Army, joined by soldiers of the First Polish Army, made a final attack on Berlin on 16 April 1945. At this point, most Nazi leaders had either already been captured or killed and the city itself had suffered severe destruction due to sustained Allied bombing. Having failed to rally civilians (including children) to fight the approaching Red Army, a delusional and paranoid Hitler fled to the Führerbunker where on 30 April 1945 he committed suicide. The German army quickly collapsed in other parts of Europe and all forces unconditionally surrendered on 7 May the following month. V-E (Victory in Europe) Day was celebrated by the Western Allies on 8 May, less than 24 hours later, while the Soviet Union celebrated Victory Day on 9 May 1945.

The Second World War saw mass destruction and loss of life on a scale never seen before throughout the world. Such were the atrocities suffered by millions, especially

Rudolf Hoess,
Kommandant of
Auschwitz from
1940 to 1943,
pictured before
facing trial.

victims of the Holocaust, that war trials were an inevitable consequence. Between 1945 and 1951 both German and Japanese officials and war personnel were tried and prosecuted for heinous war crimes. Senior German officials were prosecuted at the Nuremberg Trials while senior Japanese officials faced their fates at the Tokyo War Crimes Trial. Minor trials also took place for less senior members of each nation's war personnel.

Rise & Fall of the Nazis takes a detailed look through the use of narrative and photographs to provide a comprehensive history of the rise of Nazi Germany to power and dominance and follows their subsequent downfall and the destruction of Hitler's Germany which had left the world in ruins.

Chapter 1

The First World War, Versailles and the Weimar Republic

When what became known as the Great War began on 3 August 1914, Germany was confident of victory. The armies of the Fatherland had only to follow the carefully enumerated Schlieffen plan, smash French resistance (and that of the British, if they were foolish enough to join in) within three or four weeks, and then turn their attention, aided by their magnificent railway system, to the slowly mobilizing Red Army in the East. Crushing the armies of the Czar might take a little longer, because of the sheer scale of the terrain, but it was equally inevitable. They believed (as indeed did their opponents, all choosing to

Jubilant crowds on the Pariser Platz with the picture of Kaiser Franz Joseph at the outbreak of war and mobilization of troops in August 1914.

follow the example of the brief Franco-Prussian War rather than the elongated American Civil War) that they would be home for Christmas. So cheering crowds greeted the declaration of war, and glasses were raised to the day of glory (*Der Tag*) and Germany's long-awaited triumph. It didn't quite work out like that.

But it so nearly did. The French and the British only just managed to hold the invading German armies on the Marne, almost within sight of Paris, before a swift counter-attack to their open flank caused the Germans to retreat and brought an end to all hopes of an early ceasefire. Instead, the Western Front sank rapidly into stalemate, soldiers on both sides finding the barest shelter along four hundred miles of trenches and barbed wire, all pounded into cloying mud by endless shelling. Despite early

General Field Marshall von Hindenburg presents awards and medals to soldiers on the Western Front.

German victories over the Red Army, which was invading too hastily, and continued Soviet Union incompetence thereafter, even the War in the East lasted over three years before the impact of the Bolshevik Revolution brought hostilities to a close in late 1917.

Even though Germany could now assign all her forces to the West, the economic hardships caused by the War meant that the German people were nearing the end of their tether. British control of the seas had ensured that the blockade on imports to Germany had wreaked havoc, and submarine warfare had been unable to break the stranglehold. Army Commanders Hindenburg and Ludendorff staked everything on one last desperate onslaught before the Americans (who had entered the War in April 1917) could unleash the full might of their technology and manpower. Again, they almost succeeded, but by the late summer of 1918, the tide had turned, and Allied armies were grinding relentlessly forward. With revolutionary flourishes in the air at home, it was too much for the Germans (not to mention the Austro-Hungarians) to cope with, and they sued for peace as the autumn leaves fell.

So, famously, at the eleventh hour on the eleventh day of the eleventh month, an Armistice was signed – in effect, Germany surrendered. Europe was exhausted by the struggle, and the consequences of more than four years of carnage were considerable and widespread. In Germany, they were even more devastating, all the more so because, despite the growing realism engendered by the conflict, the nation had never seriously addressed the prospects of defeat. The major knock-on effects of the catastrophe were threefold: political, economic and psychological.

Politically, the consequences were immediately apparent. Kaiser Wilhelm II, the Hohenzollern Emperor who had ruled since the death of his father in 1890, abdicated on 28 November and was forced into exile in the Netherlands. Although he had belatedly granted some autonomy to the *Reichstag* and the Chancellor in October 1918, his abdication was still an event of seismic importance. Most of the princes, dukes and rulers of the many German states did the same. The structures of the forty-eight-year-old Prussian-dominated Empire instantly collapsed and Germany was once more a conglomeration of states, although in Berlin, the socialist Friedrich Ebert had been announced as Chancellor by Prince Max of Baden, who had been his predecessor in the liberal administration, and formed a provisional government. Immediately, mini-revolutions sprang up in many parts of Germany, notably in Berlin, Munich, the Ruhr Valley and Kiel, and there were obvious fears that the Russian Revolution, inspired by Karl Marx's Communist Manifesto, would spread westward, as Lenin (and indeed the German Marx) had intended. Some cities did set up Workers' Councils; others had done so before the War's end. However, it seemed that the German people – or, at least, most of them – did not want revolution.

There were, of course, many vicious clashes. In Berlin, the hard line Spartacists (as the Communist party was known) had originally been in league with the Independent Socialists, but they disagreed vehemently with the compromises that government forced the socialists to make, and split apart from them. Now they called a general strike as a prelude to an uprising in January 1919. The right-wing militia that was comprised of

Representatives of the Allies in front of the railway carriage in which the Armistice was signed in November 1918: at the front Marshal Ferdinand Foch and RE Wemyss.

remnants of the Army (the *Freikorps*) squashed this in its infancy, killing their charismatic leaders, Rosa Luxemburg and Karl Liebknecht, in the process. The Spartacist Revolution lasted less than two weeks. Kiel, a naval base,

saw the formation of a Workers' and Soldiers' Council,
showing that not all military bodies were reactionary by
nature. In Munich, a socialist journalist, Kurt Eisner,
announced a separate Bavarian Republic. Civil war broke
out in southern Germany as a result. Through all this
turmoil, Ebert pressed ahead with plans for reform and

German soldiers withdraw from Alsace in November 1918.

elections were held for a National Assembly, which was summoned to meet in Weimar on 6 February 1919.

Although they had been to some extent the most successful of all the nations in placing their economy on a war footing, the Germans had not been able to stave off privations indefinitely. By the winter of 1918, food was extraordinarily scarce and the Germany economy was in a complete mess. Throughout the War, the Germans had borrowed massively without pausing to count the cost, expecting to repay at leisure, as victors. They had held fond hopes that their defeated enemies would cover their debts; such hopes were extinguished. The other side of their balance of payments was in equivalent disarray. Unable to export their goods except to Austro-Hungary and Turkey, these debts had been rising massively. Now it was likely that they would have to make up losses incurred by the Allies, especially Britain and France. To find the sums to pay for both their own reconstruction and the demands of others was likely to prove crippling.

The damage to the German psyche was cataclysmic. A young nation, created by the ruthless *realpolitik* of Bismarck, had known only minor setbacks and was ill-equipped to deal with disaster. Many of their people refused to believe the facts. German armies, and their navy when it had been allowed out of harbour, had

Captured Communists are led away by *Freikorps* soldiers after the defeat of the Bavarian Soviet Republic in May 1919.

actually acquitted themselves well, they reasoned. What made it hardest for Germans to bear was the fact that these armies (apart from the ill-conceived Russian invasion in 1914 that they had so brutally destroyed at Tannenberg) had also fought the whole War on foreign soil. Even on 11 November 1918, that was still the case. This feeling of sour grapes was further nurtured by an unknown British general (who may, or may not, have actually existed) who is alleged to have remarked that the German Army had been stabbed in the back by events at home. And thus a whole legend of treachery grew up, one carefully fostered by right-wing militarists and self-styled patriots. Basically, Germans could not come to terms with the fact that they had lost and began an endless search for scapegoats and excuses.

Such feelings of discontent were scarcely improved by the news that the Germans were going to have to accept full responsibility for the War. Even though it had been clear from the terms of the Armistice that this was the case, Germans had tried to shrug away the implications, but it was a vain hope. War guilt and reparations were two of the major themes on which Allied negotiators insisted at the Paris Peace talks leading to the Treaty of Versailles. Chaired by French President Clemenceau, these negotiators took as their starting line the famous Fourteen Points set down by American President Wilson in a speech to Congress nine months after the USA entered the War in April 1917. Apart from the important last point establishing the League of Nations, the clauses mostly referred specifically to what other countries might expect as a result of peace. But the Paris talks went way beyond this – feelings had hardened by November 1918 and by the time delegates met in 1919, whipped up by rabble-rousing popular journalism ("Make Germany Pay" screamed the *Daily Mail* in London), some Allied politicians, particularly the French, were in an even more vengeful mood.

There were three main back-breaking sanctions when the terms were ratified. Article 160 stipulated that the German Army should be reduced from its bloated size (total numbers, including *Freikorps* units, were at least 600,000) to 100,000 men, a decree that wherever it was followed, merely unleashed hordes of discontented, near-uncontrollable trained killers who often promptly found employment as militia to cause havoc throughout the land. Moreover, the reduced army was almost without exception recruited from country peasants, far more likely to be anti-republican in sentiment than the enlarged army had been. The all-powerful General Staff was completely disbanded. Furthermore, there was to be no construction of tanks, artillery or military aircraft, no poison gas nor other hardware (a ban that the Germans soon got round by entering into an unholy pact with the Soviet Union to produce these jointly on Russian soil).

It wasn't just the Army and Air Force that suffered. The German Navy lost its base at Heligoland and was reduced to a rump of twelve torpedo boats, twelve destroyers, six light cruisers and six battleships. There were to be no submarines whatsoever – the British, especially, were resolved that Germany's challenge to her dominion of the seas was not to recur. Total manpower in the Navy was to be restricted to 15,000.

Second was the insistence on German guilt. Article 231 stated: "The Allied and Associated Governments affirm and Germany accepts the responsibility of Germany and

Freikorps troops with machine guns are posted on the balcony of the Adlon Hotel in Unter den Linden during the general strike of March 1919.

her allies for causing all the loss and damage to which the Allied and Associated Governments and their nationals have been subjected as a consequence of the war imposed upon them by the aggression of Germany and her allies." There was to be no escape.

Linked to this was the contentious clause on paying for this guilt. Article 232 enshrined that "compensation will be made by Germany for all damage done to the civilian population of the Allies and their property." A separate body was set up to agree the amount by 1921 and present the bill to Germany. It was inevitably huge.

This compensation was eventually fixed by the Reparations Commission in April 1921 at the staggering figure of 132,000 million gold marks (equivalent to £6,600 million) with 1,000 million marks to be paid by the end of the following month. At that rate, the Germans would be paying back instalments for at least three decades to come, ensuring that it would be the descendants of those who had gone to war who would be suffering for the sins of their fathers, as, among others, the British economist John Maynard Keynes pointed out in *The Economic Consequences of the Peace.*

The German people were bitterly resentful of these decisions, as they had been of the make-up of the Versailles Peace Conference, where they did not have a representative. They were not alone in this – neither defeated nor neutral powers were invited to send envoys to Versailles. However, many Germans had rightly suspected that their country would have to bear the brunt of the reparations. They also reckoned they would lose most territory, and were again correct in their assumptions. So they awaited the *fait accompli* with bitter fatalism.

It was even worse than they had feared. Violent outrage was caused in Germany by the not entirely unexpected, but still shattering, revelations that the revived state of Poland would be claiming two vital and linked areas from Prussia; the industrialized area of Posen

The German delegation at the Allied Peace Conference in Paris (April to June 1919).

around the city of Poznan, and the corridor leading to the port of Danzig. These were not the only areas lost to Germany, but they aroused the fiercest passions. Riots and demonstrations, particularly in Berlin, indicated the strength of national feeling.

Part of Upper Silesia went to Poland, part to Czechoslovakia. Lithuania, Latvia and Estonia (briefly German since the Treaty of Brest-Litovsk in 1918) became separate nation states. The city-port of Memel became Lithuanian, after a period of French control. The Rhineland became a demilitarized zone; Germany could not fortify the western bank nor place troops or defences in an area fifty kilometres wide on the eastern bank. This was another major bone of contention, borne – as were many of the decisions – from France's avowed desire to ruin Germany for years to come.

As well as giving back the provinces of Alsace and Lorraine to France (the same ones Germany had seized at

Foreign minister Müller and Minister of Transport Bell sign the Treaty of Versailles in the Hall of Mirrors on 28 June 1919.

Demonstrators march through Berlin's Potsdamer Strasse in November 1919 in protest at the return of Posen to Poland and the decision to make Danzig a free city under the provisions of the Treaty of Versailles.

the end of the short war in 1870), they were also required to give France the rights to the coal mines of the Saar for fifteen years. The territory was to be governed by the League of Nations for that time, on condition that there would then be a plebiscite to decide which country the

inhabitants wanted to join (in 1935, possibly overawed, they chose Germany). Another plebiscite was decreed for the people of Schleswig, an area partially overrun in 1864, where the immediate result was that the southern and central portions chose Germany and the northern parts

Phillipp Scheidemann, who would later become the first Chancellor of the new Republic, gives a speech from a window of the Reich Chancellery.

chose Denmark. Belgium received small frontier zones around Eupen and Malmedy.

In all, Germany lost one-eighth of its population and territory, one sixth of its coal industry and half its iron and steel industry. The country also had to resign all its rights and titles over widely-scattered colonies, a million square miles in total. In the Far East, they were parcelled up between New Zealand, Australia and Japan. Germany's colonies in Africa were divided between Great Britain, France and Belgium, with the exception of South-West Africa which was to be administered by the Union of South Africa. Germany's world power status had vanished overnight.

At first, the Germans refused to sign a treaty in which they had had no part. Phillipp Scheidemann resigned as Chancellor and the German Navy scuttled its own ships. The Allies were in no mood to compromise and informed Ebert that if they did not sign by 28 June 1919, the War would be rekindled. There was a body of opinion in Germany that wanted to move to call the Allies' bluff, but the stakes were far too high. Hindenburg informed Ebert that the army was in no fit state to resist and, barely four hours before the deadline, the President reluctantly signed.

Meanwhile, the elected representatives were attempting to forge a clear path for a democratic Germany back in Weimar. It was not just because it was Goethe's birthplace that they met in this quiet town, but it also avoided the hurly-burly of Berlin. The Weimar Assembly was elected on a system of proportional representation (which meant a huge increase in the number of parties) from votes potentially cast by all men and women over twenty years of age. There were 423 deputies, of whom the Majority Socialists (the less extreme of the Social Democrats) were the largest party with 165 seats, which however failed to deliver them a majority where they needed it – in the Assembly. Their leader, Scheidemann, formed a temporary alliance with members of the Catholic Centre Party (moderate conservative) and the German Democratic Party (liberal) in order to draw up a new constitution. Ebert was confirmed as the new President of the republic, still known as the Reich. Once things had quietened down in Berlin, the Assembly moved back there in May 1919, and, while still fulminating all the time about the draconian terms of Versailles, duly produced a new constitution, drafted principally by Hugo Preuss and modified in session, by the end of July, which came into being on 14 August 1919.

It was a federal Republic that emerged, as befitted a nation that consisted of so many states, but although these states kept control of local government, they were similarly bound to the principles of election through proportional representation and universal suffrage. The confusion created by Count Otto von Bismarck between the national and the Prussian governments was reduced by creating separate *Reich* and Prussian ministries as well as different *Reich* and Prussian Chancellors. The central government (*Reichstag*) had more complete power than the dissolved *Reich* because it now had control of its own finances, communications and the army (*Reichswehr*). The reconstituted *Reich* could now levy any tax, not merely indirect ones, so large numbers of tax administrators transferred from working for individual states to the new Ministry of Finance.

There was a federal council (the *Reichsrat*) which, rather like the House of Lords at Westminster, had only the ability to suspend, not create, legislation. The *Reichstag* became the sovereign legislative power and a supreme judicial court of the *Reich* was also established. Fundamental rights were guaranteed for every citizen – civic freedoms, equality before the law and economic freedoms, such as the right to join trade unions. The

principle of holding referendums was introduced. The President was to be chosen by popular vote every seven years, and would, in turn, appoint a Chancellor (a sort of prime minister), responsible to the Reichstag. Scheidemann became the first Chancellor of the new Republic. In its very formation, it can be seen that there were distinct elements of the working models of British, American, Swiss and French democracy mixed together.

Roll call and parade at the closure of the school for non-commissioned officers on 7 March 1920 as dictated by the Treaty of Versailles (Article 176).

Although this was a brave attempt to modernize German political machinery, the troubling factor was that the structure of society, with its landed hierarchy deprived merely of its imperial and aristocratic figureheads, was allowed to remain virtually intact. The Kaiser might have gone but the *Junkers* had not. It was clearly the fear of an imported Bolshevik Revolution that determined this. However, left-wing revolt was not the only threat to the

Republic, since right-wingers were soon to prove they could be just as dangerous, if not more so. In fact, all the factors that were later to destroy the Weimar Republic were present, with that ghastly inevitability of historical timing, at its birth. In the first Assembly, sixty-three deputies came from the Nationalist party and the conservative People's Party, standing for Prussian militarist and patriotic interests. But they also held

Interrogation of officers in front of the trade union building in Kiel during the Kapp *putsch* of March 1920.

themselves apart, blaming the Socialist politicians of the Republic not only for the Armistice and Germany's defeat, but for the terms of Versailles. How long would they support Weimar? They represented a significant minority opinion and, sure enough, the first attempt at a reactionary coup was not long in coming.

In the early spring of 1920, a far-right uprising known as the Kapp *putsch* took place in Berlin. Captain Ehrhardt

Internal strife in the Ruhr district between March and May 1920 saw the workers' "Red Army" fighting against the right-wing *Freikorps*.

marched 5,000 of his swastika-helmeted (its first militaristic use at the time – the Nazis adopted it later that year) marine troops, who were due to be disbanded, into the capital on 13 March and proclaimed a government headed by Wolfgang Kapp, a right-wing journalist, and General von Luttwitz. Some military forces supported them and even those loyal to the Weimar republic held back from intervening, when requested to do so by Ebert and Gustav Noske, the Defence Minister. General von Seeckt, in command of the local army detachments, said that his troops could not fire on fellow soldiers so Ebert and the government hurriedly moved to Dresden, before retreating further to Stuttgart. However, the Berlin workers refused to be overawed, declared a general strike, and crippled the city. Ironically, the most successful general strike in Germany at the time was held in support of a government rather than against one. On 16 March, the rebels, who had been reduced to inaction and were squabbling amongst themselves, threw in the towel and fled in their turn. Nearly all of these insurrectionaries escaped, however, with their lives (in marked contrast to those of most left-wing rebels).

One side effect of the failed insurrection was that General von Seeckt replaced General von Luttwitz as the chief of the *Reichswehr* – in the following year, it was to be von Seeckt who was responsible for negotiating the illegal military training and production deals with the Russians. At the same time as the Kapp *putsch* was dying on the vine, fierce fighting broke out in the Ruhr Valley where a revolution of a different stamp was under way between members of the self-styled Red Ruhr Army there and the reactionary *Freikorps*, lasting from March to May 1920. At first the Red Ruhr Army, inspired by Marchwitza, had some successes before the repression was stepped up and the workers' insurrection subsided. There was further simultaneous unrest in Kiel, Hanover and Leipzig.

"Red Army" workers familiarize themselves with a heavy machine gun in 1920, one of many weapons stolen from military depots.

Meanwhile, there had also been civil war in Bavaria, where the Bavarian Soviet Republic proclaimed by Kurt Eisner (who had only just been released from jail for treason) in Munich on 8 November 1918, had clashed bloodily with the *Freikorps*. Eisner himself, after being defeated in elections, was killed in February 1919 – on his way to make his resignation speech in the Bavarian parliament – and a Socialist government under Johannes Hoffmann took over.

Two months later the local soviets tried their hand at seizing power again in April 1919 under Ernst Toller whereupon the fledgling Socialist government fled to Bamberg, but the attempted revolution soon failed and Hoffmann returned. If it was a hotbed of left-wing sedition, Bavaria was also crammed with supporters of the Pan-German League, a right-wing nationalist organization, and other reactionary parties, who all wanted to save Germany from Communism, and remould it in the Bavarian image. These parties were swelled by decommissioned soldiers who soon took a hand.

In March 1920, Hoffmann was forced to resign again, and the right-wing knight Gustav von Kahr formed an anti-socialist coalition government that aimed to make Bavaria a Free State. This was yet another chapter in the long-standing rivalry between Munich and Berlin but the authorities in Berlin were not prepared to listen – they were also quite rightly not happy about the numbers of armed mercenaries roaming Bavaria. As part of the Treaty of Versailles, the central Government had responsibility for ensuring such militia were disarmed. Refusing to act on their orders to crack down on these gangs, a brooding Kahr himself resigned in September 1921.

One of the former soldiers (although he was not technically demobbed until March 1920) in the disbanded army who had been taking part in all these events was Adolf Hitler. He had joined the newly-formed *Deutsche Arbeiter Partei* or German Workers' Party in September 1919 – after initially being sent to investigate it on behalf of military intelligence by Captain Karl Mayr – and so impressed them that he rapidly got onto its political committee.

By 1920, the group had rebranded itself the *Nationalsozialistiche Deutsche Arbeiter Partei* (NSDAP) or National Socialist German Workers' party. It soon began to be shortened to the Nazi Party. With aims that were anti-communist, anti-parliamentary and anti-Semitic, it was

Adolf Hitler was no stranger to infiltrating crowds. He is pictured here in Munich in 1914.

Hindenburg,
Luddendorff and
Tirpitz in the
funeral
procession for the
German Empress,
Auguste Viktoria,
in April 1921.

backed by General Ludendorff and various former members of the Pan-German League and other right-wingers. Ludendorff, Hindenburg's brilliant Chief of Staff, had decamped to Sweden after persuading the politicians to sign the Armistice, but he had now returned to Bavaria. An ardent admirer presented a villa outside Munich to Ludendorff and his dotty wife, who turned it into a temple

for the cult of Wotan. Hitler, who became Chairman of the Nazi Party in July 1921, revelled in the company of these lunatic but well-connected "patriots" (the former corporal mixing with the erstwhile general) and searched around in the mayhem that was Bavaria to see what further trouble he and his followers (he had rapidly declared himself *Führer*, or Leader) could stir up.

Chapter 2

Chaos, the end of money, the Beerhall *Putsch* and key figures

Hitler, a house painter, had fancied himself as an artist. Curiously, he had been at school in Linz with Ludwig Wittgenstein, a philosopher who was also to have a great impact on the twentieth century, although perhaps not as marked as his contemporary. Needless to say, Hitler also considered himself a bit of a philosopher.

He also believed himself, with slightly more justification to be an artist. However he had twice been rejected by Vienna's Academy of Art which had wrecked what little faith he had left in his native land. Such disenchantment, along with his already developed anti-Semitism (Vienna was an important Jewish centre), his disdainful rejection of the *pot-pourri* of Austro-Hungarian society and, more immediately, his efforts to dodge the draft, caused him to flee across the border to Munich in 1913. Once there, he felt he had arrived at his spiritual home. It had not been cowardice he had displayed, he consoled himself, but an unwillingness to risk himself for an entity, the crumbling Hapsburg Empire, that he did not believe in.

One thing he proved himself to be without doubt was a soldier. Hitler joined the 16th Bavarian Reserve Infantry Regiment immediately upon outbreak of the Great War, fighting bravely on the Western Front, where he was twice wounded, severely suffered from gas attacks, won both

classes of Iron Cross and was promoted to Corporal. There is a legend that once, when wandering wounded and listless near the end of the War, he was spared from certain death by the humanity of a British soldier, who lowered his rifle. Hitler nodded vacantly and went on his way. Whether true or false, Hitler allowed this story to become part of his own myth, endlessly recycled to others, remarking that he had been spared for greater things (it was undeniable that he often had astonishing good fortune). He was to find the first of his opportunities soon enough.

Throughout the early 1920s, the reconstituted Reich continued to be a lawless place, although the major rebellions were put down. However, two of the most prominent political murders showed how close Germany was lurching towards the abyss. On 26 August 1921, Matthias Erzberger, the socialist politician who had

Hitler (back row, second from the right) convalesces with other patients at the Beelitz field hospital in October 1916.

Hitler in an open-top car with *Freikorps* officers Ulrich Graf, Major Buch and Christian Weber in 1923.

reluctantly signed the terms of the Armistice (mainly because the military authorities, possibly already mindful of their "undefeated" legend, had refused to do so) was killed. In June 1922, Walther Rathenau, the Foreign Minister who had treated with the French at Wiesbaden and signed the Treaty of Rapallo with the Soviet government the previous year, was also butchered. Significantly, he was Jewish. In neither case did the authorities pursue the murderers with anything approaching conviction, judges tending to sympathize with the views of these "patriotic" killers.

At the same time, the Germans were struggling to make the repayments as set out by the Reparations Committee. The first payment was only paid at the end of August 1921 (three months late) – there is more than a hint that it was the only one they ever stumped up in cash, although there were several payments of goods in kind.

By the beginning of 1923, Germany was hurtling into chaos. Unemployment was rising, the political situation was near to crisis at both regional and national level, and debts were still mounting. The Germans claimed that it was impossible to keep up with repayments, pointing to

The decline of the
Deutschmark (a
sample of the
notes are shown
here) was swift.

the disasters that were afflicting the mark. The French,
urged on by premier Raymond Poincaré with thoughtless
if partially understandable vindictiveness, and the
Belgians promptly occupied the Ruhr Valley. The workers
and employers there saw to it that most of the industries
ground to a halt. Their government printed money so
recklessly that devaluation, already looming, took off like
a rocket. British and American businessmen and
politicians, who had been quite happy to trade with
Germany rather than rely on reparations, watched
helplessly.

The collapse of the currency advanced with frightening
speed. In January 1923, the mark was worth 20,000 to the
US dollar. It depreciated fivefold in the next five months so
that it was worth 100,000 to the dollar by the middle of
June. Then it went into freefall. By August, a dollar was
worth five million marks; by September, it was worth fifty
million; and by November, it was worth 630,000 million.
Obviously wages and salaries, even though they were
being revised daily, could not begin to keep up with such

hyperinflation of prices. People were being paid in wheelbarrow loads of paper money, but it was essentially valueless. Everyone was desperately trying to convert their money, cash that was literally not worth the paper it was printed on, into goods. Debts were wiped out overnight, the middle class was ruined and only those with some form of tangible property survived.

There was a suspicion that the government had allowed the crisis to spiral out of control so that Germany's more voracious international creditors, such as France and

Children play with the now worthless currency in November 1923.

Hitler with Rudolf
Hoess, Emil
Maurice, Kriebel
and Christian
Weber in 1923.

Belgium, could be taught a lesson about reparations. The
result of the collapse of the mark was that a new scheme
for rescheduling the debts was hurriedly put together,
called the Dawes Plan after the American Charles Dawes,
one that after its introduction in 1924 helped to right the
predicament with surprising ease and laid the foundations
for five years of prosperity until the crash of 1929. It did
this because it reorganized the *Reichsbank*, set up loans, and
evacuated the Ruhr – in short, it provided the basis for re-
stabilizing the German economy which suddenly entered
a boom period after its apparently apocalyptic times of
bust. Hence overseas observers suspected things maybe

hadn't been quite as bad as they were allowed to appear. This is not to say that many people in Germany did not suffer grievously. The reparation debts may have been rescheduled, but there is no evidence that the Germans ever actually paid any of the supposed regular sums. So, in the final analysis, all that the reparations did was to cause untold difficulties and huge, lingering resentment. On that, at least, Keynes was right.

But there was another legacy of the currency crisis of 1923. The loss of confidence which it had engendered in all German people, and especially in the middle classes, had become endemic – and this was not so easily restored. There is a direct link between the failing of the Weimar Republic to solve this problem, however much they might have half-greeted it, and the rise of the extremist right-wing Nazis. A stronger middle class would have acted as a natural bulwark against them.

Amid all this chaos, Hitler decided to support the mounting of a right-wing coup in Munich. The original leaders of this planned coup were Kahr (two years after he had resigned as Bavarian President), Seisser and Lossow who had decided that they would stage their uprising in mid-November, but got cold feet and postponed their enterprise on 4 November. Maddened, Hitler decided to force the issue. With members of his Nazi party he surrounded and occupied the Beerhall in Munich where the three conspirators were meeting on 8 November, and compelled them to reconsider. Having done so with indecent haste, Kahr escaped with even greater alacrity and raised the alarm. The following day, detachments from the Army met the rebels as they marched to secure key buildings in Munich.

Hitler was too far ahead of the game. He had counted on the fragility of the Bavarian Government and that, mindful of this, the detachments from the Reichswehr would support him. Unfortunately for him, the government had grown stronger, demonstrated that it was not prepared to be pushed around, and the soldiers reacted accordingly. However sympathetic some of the officers and troops may have been to Hitler's aims, they

recognized that the time was not right for a rightist insurrection. It was not a long battle – one volley from the troops, and the Nazis surrendered, leaving sixteen dead on the streets. The *putsch* had failed.

However, Hitler cunningly used the circumstances of the trial in March 1924 to turn abject defeat into some form of victory. He answered questions about the fiasco with long speeches that set forth his political views and

Members of Hitler's *putsch* of 8–9 November 1923.

Rise & Fall of the Nazis

Following his failed *putsch*, Hitler was put on trial for treason in Munich in February 1924. The defendants (Hitler, Ludendorff, Roehm, Frick, Kriebel et al) are pictured here in front of the building of the former military school in the Blutenburgstrasse, where the trial was held.

LUDENDORFF   HITLER   RÖHM   FRICK   KOHLER

BRÜCKNER   WAGNER

RODER SCHRAMM   ZEZSCHWITZ

LÜTJEBRUNE   PERNET   SCHRAMM

Hitler reading in
Landsberg prison.

instantly made him a champion of the far right. It had been difficult to stand out from the crowd of self-styled saviours of Germany but this was an effective way of doing so. The mundane trappings of the *putsch* were elevated through his strident rhetoric into the heroic realms of a great, doomed enterprise. Despite this well-trodden method of playing to the gallery, he was found guilty.

Even his spell in Landsberg Prison did not prove particularly arduous. Hitler had been sentenced to five years in jail, but he only served nine months. Landsberg is a small Bavarian town on the river Lech, and he found himself among friends and fellow travellers. During that time he dictated the words of the notorious book that would serve as the foundation stone of his political philosophy, such as it was.

Mein Kampf was an almost unreadable splurge, a combination of self-romanticism and vicious outpourings of hatred that nevertheless went on to exert a powerful influence on many of Hitler's followers. It also served as a blueprint for what Hitler intended to do – in the years to come he carried out (or attempted) nearly all of the rabid threats contained in its many pages. As such, it is an important testament.

It was during the days leading to the *putsch* and thereafter that Hitler started to gather together some of the men who were to become crucial in the rise and life of the Nazi party.

One of the people who had been at his side in prison (and indeed had enjoyed the dubious privilege of listening to the future Führer dictate his manifesto) was Rudolf Hoess, who scribbled it down dutifully. Born in Alexandria in Egypt in 1894, the son of a rich exporter, he fought as a

Ernst Roehm and Rudolf Hoess, pictured in 1933.

soldier and an airman in the Great War. Afterwards he joined the *Freikorps* to help put down the Communist uprisings. Hearing Hitler speak in Munich in 1920, he signed up at once, the sixteenth to become a card-carrying member of the party. After emerging from prison, he continued his activities, working as Hitler's secretary. In 1932, his unofficial status ended, and he was made a general in the SS, and, the following year, Deputy Führer. It was an almost entirely ceremonial position due to his inability to think for himself or carry on political intrigues (not lacking in other members of the Nazi party). Famously, Hoess flew to Britain in May 1941 with an offer of peace, but most observers, including Churchill, concluded he had gone mad. Sentenced to life imprisonment at Nuremberg, he lived on for many years before he committed suicide in Spandau Jail in 1987.

Every would-be dictator needs a thuggish strong-arm man, and Hitler found his in Ernst Roehm. Born in 1887 in Munich, Roehm had fought ferociously during the War, even when he had been wounded three times, and continued to do so as a commander in the *Freikorps*. Another who joined the nascent Nazi party in 1920, he was similarly involved in the Beerhall *putsch* in 1923. After serving 15 months in Landsberg, much of it with Hitler, he fell out with him soon after release, and went to Bolivia. However, Hitler seduced him back and he eventually became leader of the *Sturm Abteilung* (SA), the self-styled brown shirts, when the banned organization, which he had originally helped to found, was resuscitated. Its titular head, Hitler, chose initially to turn a blind eye to the hard drinking and homosexual orgies (the Nazis were by no means broad-minded) for which the SA became notorious.

Joseph Goebbels
would prove to be
influential in the
new Nazi
Germany.

Other differences remained – Roehm was a genuine socialist who disapproved of the overtures to capitalist interests and the army which Hitler found necessary to secure power. He was murdered in a Munich prison two days after his troops had been butchered in the Night of the Long Knives on 30 June 1934 at Bad Wiessee.

But even more than thugs (who could basically be whistled up from anywhere, and often were) Hitler was smart enough to realize that he needed a good propagandist and found one in Joseph Goebbels. Born in Reydt in the Rhineland in 1897, Goebbels did not fight in the War owing to a club foot, a fact about which he was exceedingly sensitive. Instead he received a doctorate of philosophy from Heidelberg University. He joined the Nazi party in 1924, and was assigned to Berlin to build up support there. He was so successful in this that he was made head of the Nazi propaganda machine in 1929. After Hitler became Chancellor, he was appointed Minister of Propaganda and Enlightenment, and stayed in his post until the end. He was an expert in his craft and certainly fooled the majority of the German people and much of Europe, at least until it was too late to do much about it. A staunch supporter of family values in public, he was an inveterate womaniser in private. He also died in the Bunker on 1 May 1945.

The nearest that the Nazis came to a person with social cachet was Hermann Goering. Born in Rosenheim in 1893, he was the son of a judge and joined the army in 1914. He ended the Great War as one of the principal German air

Hermann Goering, pictured circa 1923 in SA uniform.

aces, in charge of the von Richthofen squadron, and festooned with Iron Crosses. Afterwards, he toured Scandinavia in a flying circus, meeting his first wife, Baroness Karin von Fock-Kantzow, whom he married in Munich in 1922. Hitler asked him to command the SA in the same year, and he took part in the Beerhall *putsch*, during which he was badly wounded. He fled the country and recovered in hospital and an asylum in Sweden, becoming addicted to morphine in the process. Returning to Germany in 1927, he was elected to the *Reichstag* the following year, and used his contacts book to help Hitler's rise to power. Once in office in 1933, he became Minister for Aviation, Chief of the Prussian Police and the Gestapo and Prussian Minister of the Interior. He helped plan the eclipse of Ernst Roehm and took over as Commander in Chief of the Air Force in 1935. Vain, and an incorrigible showman, he basked in Germany's successes in the late 1930s and 1940 but he was unable to cope with reverses,

Goering, as commander of the von Richthofen squadron, in the cockpit of his fighter plane circa 1918.

Eva Braun would be Hitler's companion for thirteen years before their death.

and lost confidence after defeats in The Battle of Britain and on the Russian front. Nevertheless, he was foremost in planning concentration camps and the Final Solution. Unable to face justice, he took poison at Nuremberg in 1946.

In Hitler's conception of Germany, there was precious little room for women, apart from child-rearing, in the kitchen and at church (*Kinder, Küche, Kirche*). He made an exception for a striking Bavarian blonde, however, Eva Braun, whom he met in 1929, when she was working for the official Nazi party photographer. Born in Munich in February 1912, Eva was the daughter of a middle-class schoolteacher and a respectable if long-suffering mother. Her affair with Hitler was fraught, involving several suicide attempts (a besetting problem for many of Hitler's women), before it settled down to a strange mixture of occasional cosy domesticity and an approximation of in-house arrest. Hitler's chauffeur reckoned she was the unhappiest woman in the *Reich*. Apparently she also had a love of nude sunbathing that used to drive her fastidious protector wild with rage. Never remotely a political influence, her very existence was kept secret from the vast majority of people in the country and it remains an enigma as to how much she actually knew about what was going on in Germany. Derided by some as empty-headed, she refused to leave Hitler near the end. She was to commit suicide with him on 30 April 1945 just after a hurried celebration of marriage and just before the Russians stormed his bunker in Berlin.

The son of a schoolteacher, Heinrich Himmler, became one of the most powerful men in Nazi Germany. Born in Munich in 1900, he was just young enough to serve in the army at the end of the Great War. Soon afterwards, he joined the Nazi party and took part in the Munich Beerhall *putsch*, characteristically evading arrest. In 1927, he was appointed to be Deputy Commander of the *Schutzstaffel* (SS) and, two years later, its Commander, where he was instrumental in manoeuvring the black shirts, Hitler's bodyguard, away from the SA, under whose larger banner they were marching at that time.

By 1933, as the Nazis took power, SS membership had swelled from 280 to 52,000 – a battle royal with the SA was looming. Himmler, Heydrich and cohorts such as Goering and Blomberg were successful in the Night of the Long

Heinrich Himmler, leader of the SS, pictured in 1933.

Knives. That same year, 1934, he took control of the Gestapo and founded Germany's first concentration camp. He must take large responsibility for the development of the Final Solution, the extermination of Jews. Wildly anti-Semitic, he used all sorts of crackpot theories to justify his hideous repressions, but despite having fierce rivals, such as Martin Bormann, he remained in the upper echelons of the Nazis until the final conflagration. He committed suicide after being captured following the end of the War in 1945.

One of the main architects of the Final Solution was Reinhard Heydrich. Born in Halle in 1904, the son of highly musical parents in that excessively musical Saxon city, he survived slurs against his possibly Jewish background and expulsion from the Navy for "conduct unbecoming an officer and a gentleman" in 1931, to join the Nazi party at the suggestion of his somewhat forgiving new wife (the misconduct is thought to have been in matters of a sexual nature). Heydrich was supremely ruthless and coldly impersonal, even by Nazi standards, and Himmler immediately appointed him to be the head

Reinhard
Heydrich.

of the *Sicherheitsdienst* (SD), the counter-intelligence unit of the SS. In this capacity, he was responsible for setting up the first concentration camp at Dachau when the Nazis came to power. When the SD was merged with the Gestapo in 1936, he assumed control of the camp and gradually came to be regarded as Himmler's right-hand man, indispensable if boundlessly arrogant and prickly. Heydrich organized the infamous Wannsee Conference early in 1942, where the plans for the Final Solution were discussed in detail. Shot on his way to his office in Prague in May 1942, he died from his wounds a week later. Hitler, who had been considering him as a possible successor, ordered a state funeral and vicious reprisals.

The main executor of Heydrich's policies was Adolf Eichmann. Born in Solingen in 1906, the son of an industrialist, he worked for his father's mining company in Linz and did other desultory jobs in Austria before returning to Germany in 1933, after the Nazis had come to power. He had already joined the party in Austria and rapidly rose up the hierarchy, forming the SS's Central Office of Jewish Emigration in 1938 and touring the Middle East trying to offload Germany's "Jewish Problem". However his career progression stalled at a certain point, just below the rank of full Colonel, which later allowed him to use the classic defence that he was "only obeying orders". Heydrich ordered him to attend the notorious Wannsee Conference in January 1942 and he was then put in charge of transport towards the Final Solution. After the occupation of Hungary he ordered 400,000 to their deaths in the gas chambers. At the end of the war, he managed to escape from US custody and, five years later, he made his way to Argentina. Eventually he was tracked

Josef Mengele.

down by Israeli agents, captured and taken back for trial.
Found guilty, he was hanged in Israel in 1962.

After the Nazis had grown even more deranged with
power, and their notorious Final Solution programme had
begun, there was a call for promising doctors who were
ideologically sound. The most feared of these became Josef
Mengele, a former SA member who had resigned and

joined the SS in 1938. Born in Gunzburg, Bavaria in 1911, he was the son of an industrial magnate, who graduated in medicine from Munich University in 1935 and received a doctorate (later withdrawn) from Frankfurt in 1938 for his racially-motivated research. He fought on the Eastern Front, before being invalided out of his SS regiment, receiving the Iron Cross to soothe his wounds. He took up a post as one of the camp doctors in Auschwitz, where his sadistic and revolting experiments earned him the nickname of The Angel of Death, standing out even from a crowd of like-minded murderers. Although not in charge, he was chillingly pre-eminent. Amazingly he managed to escape the net at the end of the War, and was smuggled to South America. He finally died in Brazil in 1979.

Walter Rauff was guilty of causing 100,000 deaths personally in his capacity as a Colonel in the SS during the Second World War. Born in Koethen in 1907, he joined up

Walter Rauff.

as a naval cadet in 1924. He had been a friend of Heydrich in the German Navy and, when he resigned from his own command in 1937, his old comrade hired him to put the SS and the SD onto a war footing. Basically this meant developing mobile gas chambers to kill Jews, Communists and other enemies of the German state. Rauff embraced his task enthusiastically. After a wartime career which, like that of his mentor, outstripped even most other Nazis for callous indifference to human life, especially in North Africa and Italy, he managed to escape in 1945. For a while, Rauff worked in intelligence in the Middle East, before following the well-worn trail to South America. He was tracked down and, although he freely admitted to his crimes and was signally unrepentant, the Pinochet regime in Chile would not let him return to face his accusers. He died in Chile in 1984.

Albert Speer was born in Mannheim in 1905, and studied to become an architect, like his father and grandfather, at Karlsruhe, Munich and Berlin. In 1930 he attended a couple of Nazi rallies and was deeply impressed by Hitler's speeches, joining the party immediately. Within two years, he had helped Troost redevelop the Chancellery, impressing Hitler in the process, and within four, on Troost's death, he had become the Nazi party architect, unfurling inflated Greek designs on the vast Nuremberg parade grounds. Hitler's epic megalomania ensured that Speer was never short of projects (although many remained at the planning stage) such as the stadium for the Berlin Olympics. In 1942, he was made Minister of Armaments when Fritz Todt was killed in an aeroplane crash, and proved surprisingly successful, quadrupling production. At the trials in

Nuremberg, he was one of the few who admitted guilt, asked for forgiveness and was consequently spared, spending 20 years in Spandau Prison. He died in London in 1981.

Albert Speer.

One of the few theologians who had the courage of his convictions and stood up to Hitler was the Protestant pastor Dietrich Bonhoeffer. Born at Breslau, a suburb of Berlin, in 1906, he had become a Lutheran priest in 1931 and, after four years in England, returned to Germany and continually raised his voice against the Nazis and, in particular, their anti-Semitism. A pillar of the confessing church, he wrote thirty-nine books to back up his beliefs. He was arrested in 1943 and executed in the concentration camp at Flossenburg in April 1945 for his part in a plot to assassinate Hitler, links having been found between him and the Military Intelligence officers involved.

Chapter 3

Adolf Hitler and his personal rise to power

The transformation of Adolf Hitler from a drifter with no formal educational qualifications and no aim in life into a charismatic, dictatorial individual who galvanised a country defeated in the First World War and made it believe it could not only recover its former glory but conquer its hated enemies is astonishing.

Adolf Hitler's father was born Alois Schicklgruber in 1837. He died in 1903.

Klara Pölzl, Alois' third wife and Adolf's mother, was born in 1860 and died in 1907.

Strangely, the man who would become Germany's leader actually hailed from nearby Austria. It was also ironic that a man who would one day lead a movement that placed the greatest importance on a person's family tree and antecedents came from a very mixed background.

His father, Alois, was born in 1837, the illegitimate son of Maria Anna Schicklgruber. Maria was employed as a cook by a wealthy Jewish family named Frankenberger, and it's not impossible their 19-year-old son was Adolf Hitler's grandfather.

When Alois was five years old, Maria Schicklgruber wed Johann Hiedler, their marriage ending with her death from natural causes five years later. Alois then went to live on a farm with his uncle and was persuaded by him to stop using the last name of his mother, Schicklgruber, and change it to match his uncle's. Over the course of time Hiedler came to be spelled as Hitler.

By the time Adolf Hitler was born in Braunau am Inn, an Austro-German border town, on 20 April 1889, Alois had worked himself up the promotion tree of the Austrian civil service to become Senior Assistant Inspector in the

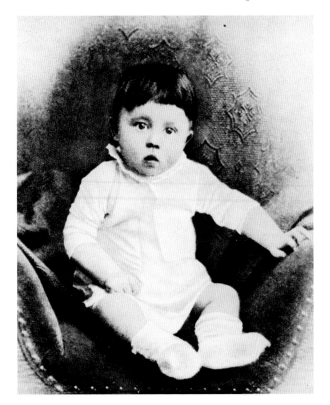

Adolf Hitler pictured in 1891. No-one could have predicted the impact that this toddler would have on world history when he grew up.

customs service. The former Klara Pölzl, Adolf's mother, was his third wife and was twenty-three years younger than her husband. She was pregnant at the time they married and, as she was Alois' niece, permission to marry had to be obtained from the Catholic Church. They would have five children together, only two of whom, Adolf and his younger sister Paula would survive into adulthood. Two siblings died from diphtheria and one died shortly after birth.

Alois had made a success of his life from modest beginnings, but his life outside work had been stormy. He had a son, Alois Jr, from a previous marriage who left home age 13 after disagreements with his father, and Adolf was expected to do far better. Unfortunately their relationship was also not a good one and regular beatings resulted. That said, Adolf was a promising pupil at his first school and, having been confirmed in the Catholic Church, was religious enough to consider becoming a monk in later life.

The Hitlers moved frequently, to Passau inside the Bavarian border in 1892 and Lambach in 1895 when Alois retired from his job. By the time Adolf got to high school in 1900 the family had moved to Linz. Alois wanted his son to follow in his career footsteps, but he rebelled and started to fail at his schoolwork, especially since he was no longer guaranteed to finish top of the class. Also, although he wanted to pursue a career in art, his father sent him to a technical school to which he was unsuited. "I thought that once my father saw what little progress I was making (at the technical school) he would let me devote myself to the happiness I dreamed of," Hitler later explained in his autobiographical book, *Mein Kampf*.

The class photo of Year 4 in Leonding. In the top row, middle, Adolf Hitler aged ten years.

It's been suggested that coming into conflict with an intellectually superior group of Jewish students, including Wittgenstein, helped inspire his anti-Semitic views.

Hitler began his second year at high school as the oldest boy in his class, having been kept back due to poor academic performance. This gave him an age advantage over his classmates and he took the opportunity to become ringleader of the younger pupils. He enjoyed re-enacting battles from the recent Boer War, especially playing the role of a commando rescuing Boers from English concentration camps.

Another of his loves was opera, especially those of German composer Richard Wagner. Hitler was captivated by his Germanic music, and the myths and legends of ancient Kings and Knights battling against hated enemies.

Leopold Pötsch, his history master, was a German Nationalist and told Hitler and his fellow pupils all about the German victories over France in 1870 and 1871. "It was not long before the great historic struggle had become my greatest spiritual experience," Hitler stated in *Mein Kampf*. "From then on, I became more and more enthusiastic about everything that was in any way connected with war or, for that matter, with soldiering." Otto von Bismarck, the first chancellor of the German Empire, was one of Hitler's early historical heroes. His other love alongside history was art, for which he showed a talent, and he had a keen interest in architecture.

Having transferred to a school at Steyr due to poor results, Hitler dropped out at 16, his father having died a couple of years earlier in 1903, of lung cancer. He had persuaded his mother to let him leave, using poor health

The philosopher Ludwig Wittgenstein (bottom left) photographed at the Realschule in Linz in 1903 together with Adolf Hitler (top right) when both boys would have been fourteen or fifteen years old.

as his excuse, and from now on would be self-taught; he was an avid reader. A celebratory drink on leaving the academic life behind proved to have unpleasant consequences; he was woken up at the side of the road next morning by a milk delivery person and, severely hung over, vowed never to touch alcohol again.

Hitler as a lance-corporal in a Bavarian volunteer regiment in the First World War, 1914.

In the spring of 1906 Hitler headed for Vienna, where he effectively began his adult life. He harboured vague ambitions to become an architect even though he lacked any formal qualifications. He augmented his family's allowance by selling paintings to tourists. He tried to make a living through art, but attempts to enrol in the city's Academy of Fine Arts were unsuccessful and he found himself in a hostel for homeless men.

The poverty he suffered in this phase of his life deeply influenced Hitler, whose lack of kindness and compassion was an enduring attitude. "I owe it to that period that I grew hard and am still capable of being hard," he stated in *Mein Kampf*.

He found himself unable to tell his mother of his dire straits, and she died of cancer in 1907 believing him to be a successful art student. Her death affected him greatly; it's said he carried her photograph wherever he went. In October 1908, he tried for a second time to gain admission to the Vienna Academy of Fine Arts but his efforts were so poor that he was not even allowed to take the formal exam. It was a bitter disappointment to him.

Inheriting his father's civil service pension as the eldest child of the family, Hitler was now relatively well off so did not have to find employment. He spent a typical morning in bed reading and in the afternoon walked around Vienna studying buildings, visiting museums and making sketches.

At the age of twenty-one, he found himself becoming interested in politics, and Vienna was a fascinating melting pot of nationalities, religions and ideologies. He closely studied the workers' party, the Social Democrats and their ability to organise large rallies and use propaganda and fear as political weapons. Other parties preached anti-Semitism and, as Vienna's population of two million included just under two hundred thousand Jews; there was plenty of food for thought.

Up until this time, however, Hitler does not appear to have been particularly hostile to Jews, on a personal level, at any rate. In fact many of his closest associates in the men's hostel, who had helped him sell his pictures when he was reduced to eating at charity soup-kitchens, were Jewish.

Hitler was called up for military service with the Austrian Army in 1909 but despised the country for not having sided with Germany against France in 1870 and 1871. He ignored the call-up papers, and four years later was arrested and extradited to Salzburg. He appealed on the grounds of poor health and successfully escaped conscription, as he was "Unfit for combatant and auxiliary duty – too weak. Unable to bear arms."

Hitler was one of many gathered in a big public plaza in Munich to celebrate the German proclamation of war on 1 August 1914. He later claimed that when he heard the news, "I was overcome with impetuous enthusiasm, and falling on my knees, wholeheartedly thanked Heaven that I had been granted the happiness to live at this time. For me, as for every German, there now began the greatest and most unforgettable time of my earthly existence. Compared to the events of this gigantic struggle, everything past receded to shallow nothingness."

Standards being less stringent in times of conflict, he was accepted to serve in the German Army as a runner for the 16th Bavarian Reserve Regiment, carrying important messages from regimental headquarters to the front line.

He moved to the Western Front a couple of months later and would serve in both France and Belgium, winning the Iron Cross.

Adolf Hitler (front left) with his fellow soldiers at the Front in the First World War.

He appears to have lived something of a charmed life. While 2,500 of the 3,000 men in the Hitler's regiment were killed, wounded or missing, he escaped without a scratch – initially, at least. But the chaos of war gave his life much-needed form and purpose.

His commanding officer wrote: "As a dispatch-runner, he has shown cold-blooded courage and exemplary boldness. Under conditions of great peril, when all the communication lines were cut, the untiring and fearless activity of Hitler made it possible for important messages to go through".

That said, he was not liked by his fellow soldiers, who

A portrait of Hitler
dating from 1921.

described him as "odd" and "peculiar". He was an isolated
figure who broke his silence only to condemn Jews and
Marxists who, he claimed, were undermining the war
effort at home.

Hitler's luck regarding injury ran out when he received
a leg wound in 1916. Assigned to light duty in Munich, he
was so shocked at the apathy and anti-war sentiment
among German civilians that he asked to return to the
front. Two years later he was hospitalized after being
caught in a gas attack. While he was in hospital Germany

surrendered and the war ended. Hitler promptly entered a state of deep depression. "There followed terrible days and even worse nights," he recalled in *Mein Kampf*. "I knew that all was lost…in these nights hatred grew in me, hatred for those responsible for this deed."

Hitler remained in the forces after the war, as under the terms of the armistice, the German Army was not disbanded but limited to a greatly reduced strength of 100,000. Though he was not considered officer material and remained at the lowly rank of corporal, Hitler had finally found a satisfactory way to live his life. The rules of military discipline, uncontested loyalty and obedience, individuals fighting for a common goal, were those he would use in later running the Nazi party.

Germany, now theoretically a republic, was in ferment, with left-wing groups constantly clashing with right-wing nationalist *Freikorps* (small armies of ex-soldiers for hire) and regular army troops. While Hitler was stationed in Munich, the capital of Bavaria, the Independent Socialist Party declared Bavaria a republic. He was appalled and, after the German Army entered Munich and overthrew the Bavarian Socialist Republic in May 1919 he unashamedly played a part in identifying fellow soldiers who had been sympathetic to the rebellion, condemning them to an unfortunate end.

He could see the need for strong leadership to reunite the once proud citizens of his country. But as a German Nationalist he opposed the socialist belief in equality. Furthermore he linked socialism with the Jewish faith as, given their past persecution, they were understandably attracted to a movement that treated all as equals. Indeed, Marx and Trotsky were Jews.

Hitler became an undercover agent in the German Army, investigating subversive political organizations and attempting to counteract the appeal of the Russian Revolution. A political indoctrination course held at the University of Munich gave him the chance to shine. He described it in *Mein Kampf*: "One day I asked for the floor. One of the participants felt obliged to break a lance for the Jews and began to defend them in lengthy arguments. This aroused me to an answer. The overwhelming majority of the students present took my standpoint. The result was that a few days later I was sent into a Munich regiment as a so-called educational officer."

His public speaking skills were now undoubted (an army report on Hitler referred to him as "a born orator") and by his discharge in 1920 Hitler had already started attending meetings of the German Workers Party (DAP), the forerunner of the Nazi Party. Ironically he had been asked to investigate it by the army but, on closer inspection, had seen the DAP as his ideal entry point into politics at the relatively advanced age of thirty.

"This absurd little organization with its few members," he recalled, "seemed to me to possess the one advantage that it had not frozen into an 'organization' but left the individual opportunity for real personal activity. Here it was still possible to work, and the smaller the movement, the more readily it could be put into the proper form. Here, the content, the goal, and the road could still be determined…"

Hitler was such a charismatic figure that he was immediately asked to join the executive committee and later appointed the party's propaganda manager. "I finally came to the conviction that I had to take this step...It was the most decisive resolve of my life. From here there was and could be no turning back."

Along with the party's founder, Anton Drexler, he wrote a twenty-five-point programme encapsulating their beliefs. They refused to accept the humiliating Treaty of Versailles, which had stripped Germany of its overseas colonies and divided its various territories, as well as shouldering a bill that amounted to nearly forty per cent of the national wealth. They believed that Germany should be reunited in a greater German Reich under a strong central government for the execution of effective legislation. The majority of the working class were unhappy enough to share these views.

The DAP was one of several nationalist parties around at the time. They also espoused socialist principles in favouring nationalization of big companies and the sharing of profits with the workforce. The last, and most sinister of all the beliefs was that non-German people, and especially Jews were blamed for many of the country's

Adolf Hitler could have an audience eating out of the palm of his hand and was very demonstrative during his orations, as this series of pictures show.

Hitler's choice of flag would soon become the most recognisable in the world. Here, the flags are paraded after being consecrated at the first Reich party convention of the NSDAP in Munich, January 1923.

problems and classed as *untermenschen* or lesser people. No Jew would henceforth be considered a German. Such policies quickly attracted support from citizens of a humiliated, beaten country, and Hitler's barnstorming speeches quickly made him a focal point of the party. His first meeting in 1919 had seen him hold the floor with his oratory, as he described in *Mein Kampf*: "I spoke for thirty minutes, and what before I had simply felt within me,

without in any way knowing it, was now proved by reality: I could speak! After thirty minutes the people in the small room were electrified and the enthusiasm was first expressed by the fact that my appeal to the self-sacrifice of those present led to the donation of three hundred marks."

Hitler also understood the need for a symbol or flag behind which the party could rally, and chose the swastika. Originally an ancient religious symbol, he placed it inside a white circle on a red background and it provided a powerful recognition point. As he explained, the choice of design was deliberate: "In the red we see the social idea of the movement, in the white the national idea, in the swastika the mission to struggle for the victory of Aryan man and at the same time the victory of the idea of creative

Hitler was revered so much that gymnasts from the German squad laid wreaths on the grave of his parents in Leonding in 1938.

work, which is eternally anti-Semitic and will always be anti-Semitic." In early 1921, Hitler spoke to a crowd of nearly six thousand in Munich, publicizing his appearance by having Party supporters drive around in swastika-decorated vehicles, throwing out leaflets for passers-by to read – direct methods that proved very effective. But Hitler's tactics were very much centred on himself as a

Hitler as a speaker at a mass rally. This colour print, based on a drawing, was displayed in German schools.

dictatorial leader, and that would prove both a strength and an Achilles heel. He saw himself as a political evangelist seeking to convert the German people to his "world view" as much as a leader, and it was the hero worship of his supporters that encouraged him to pursue his course towards dictatorship.

The summer of 1921 saw him survive a revolt among the DAP leadership in Munich when the executive committee, considering Hitler to be unacceptably overbearing, formed an alliance with a group of socialists from Augsburg. At the same time an anonymous pamphlet appeared entitled: "Adolf Hitler: Is he a Traitor?" criticizing his leadership style and the violent tactics he and his henchmen favoured.

Hitler responded to its publication in a Munich newspaper by suing for libel and later won a small amount of damages. He resigned from the party but offered to return on condition that he received unswerving loyalty and what amounted to dictatorial powers. Hitler's demands were accepted by party members by 543 votes to one and he became the leader of the party, replacing Anton Drexler. Its name was changed to National Socialist German Workers Party, more usually known as NSDAP or the Nazis. At the next meeting in July 1921, Hitler was introduced as Führer, the first time the title was publicly used.

Though Hitler did not approve of socialism per se, he redefined the word by placing the word "National" before it. Equality was only to apply to those who had "German blood"; Jews and other "aliens" would lose their rights of citizenship, and immigration by non-Germans should be ended. It would take a dozen years for him to transform the party into one of government, and there would inevitably be false steps along the way.

Impressed by Mussolini's march on Rome, Hitler resolved to seize power in Germany in similar fashion. But his first attempt in 1923 was to prove unsuccessful. It was far from the first attempt to seize control of Weimar Germany, reflecting the fact that the coalition Weimar government had gathered less than half of the seats available, but, like those before it, was doomed to failure. The Italian revolution had the support of the Italian king, so was unopposed by the army; this was not the case in Germany.

The muscle behind Hitler's rise was his *Sturm Abteilung*, or Storm Division These so-called stormtroopers attacked Jews and people who opposed him. Many opponents kept quiet simply because they were scared of

Hitler's proclamation of 9 November 1923 declared the Reich government deposed.

Proklamation
an das deutsche Volk!
Die Regierung der November-verbrecher in Berlin ist heute für abgesetzt erklärt worden.
Eine
provisorische deutsche Nationalregierung
ist gebildet worden, diese besteht aus
Gen. Ludendorff
Ad. Hitler, Gen. v. Lossow
Obst. v. Seisser

being murdered – and, if they were, the judges simply let the stormtroopers go free. By October 1923, the *Sturm Abteilung* numbered 15,000, and had a number of guns and rifles. Hitler's unsuccessful coup attempt in November 1923 came at the end of a terrible year for the country. It began with an invasion of the Rhineland by France and Belgium after Germany had fallen behind with reparation payments to those countries, and continued with rampant inflation. This would be a low point for Germany.

The coup relied on the backing of Gustav von Kahr, Bavaria's ruler, and General von Lossow, the head of the Bavarian military. Hitler planned on forming a new government with wartime General Erich Ludendorff as its figurehead. He believed that by taking control of the government of Bavaria he would then be able to extend his influence to the rest of Germany. At this point, he still believed a figurehead like the respected Ludendorff would be necessary to achieve necessary levels of support; he of course saw himself pulling the strings.

Hitler in traditional dress during his imprisonment in Landberg Fortress.

When, on 8 November 1923, Hitler and his Storm Division stormed a public meeting headed by Kahr in the Beer Hall *putsch* outside of Munich, he announced his new government. But Kahr reneged on the deal and when Ludendorff finally persuaded Hitler to lead a march through the streets, the police fired on the marchers. Unable to reach the Bavarian War Ministry to overthrow the Bavarian government and start their March on Berlin, the Nazis dispersed in confusion. Hitler was arrested two days later.

With his five year sentence for treason, he used this time to write his book *Mein Kampf* ("My Struggle") which had found an audience created during his trial when he had used his defence to elevate his profile and expound his principles. The book was dictated to his deputy Rudolf Hoess and published in two volumes in 1925 and 1926. In *Mein Kampf*, Hitler stated, "All the human culture, all the results of art, science, and technology that we see before us today, are almost exclusively the creative product of the Aryan..." Hitler blamed Jews for corrupting ethical

Title page for the 1938 edition of Hitler's *Mein Kampf* ("My Struggle") by which time it had been reprinted more than 350 times.

This meeting of the NSDAP in February 1925 shows Hitler flanked by Gregor Strasser and Himmler on his left while Rosenberg, Buch and Schwartz are on his right.

and national values, and claimed that only through dictatorship could Germany be saved from Communism and Jewish treason. "By defending myself against the Jews," he said, "I am doing the Lord's work."

Hitler's determination to lead his country stemmed from the feeling of having been stabbed in the back by the right wing establishment. This, he believed, was what he had been born for, and that determination never wavered. Hitler confessed to wanting to overthrow the government, saying he was no traitor but a German patriot and that the democratic government were the criminals. He considered the traitors of 1918 to be the German politicians who had ended the First World War prematurely and established the German democratic republic. Germany did not lose on the battlefield, but had been undermined by political treachery at home.

When Hitler was released from prison in December 1924, after serving just over a year (his nine months, plus a further three on remand), the Germany he found was different from the one he'd known in 1923. The economy had begun to improve, the infant German democratic system had begun to work and the extreme solutions proposed by Hitler seemed much less appealing than previously.

Hitler was banned from public speeches as a condition of his release so appointed Gregor Strasser to organize the party in northern Germany. Strasser, with brother Otto and Joseph Goebbels, emphasised the socialist element in the party's programme, but was defeated at the Bamberg Conference in 1926, at which time Goebbels joined Hitler on the right wing. By 1930, Hitler was back in front line politics. His speeches typically began in a low voice which gradually increased in power and authority. He promised something for everyone – work for the unemployed, prosperity for businessmen, expansion of the army, social harmony and the return of Germany's long-lost national status.

Two short-term factors finally brought Hitler to ultimate power; the first was the worldwide Economic Depression. After the Wall Street Crash of 1929, the United States called in its loans to Germany, and the country's economy collapsed. People starved on the streets, unemployment grew exponentially and in the crisis, people wanted someone to blame. They looked to the extreme solutions Hitler offered, and Nazi success in the elections grew. The number of Nazi seats in the Reichstag rose from twelve in 1928 to 230 in July 1932. The second factor was a desperate misjudgement by President Hindenburg. The Nazis failed to get a majority of seats in the Reichstag in the November 1932 elections and their share of the vote actually fell from 230 seats to only 196. Hitler was disconsolate and even contemplated suicide. But then he was rescued by Franz von Papen, a friend of Hindenburg who was Chancellor. He could not get enough support in the Reichstag to rule and was governing by emergency decree under Article 48 of the Constitution. He offered Hitler the post of vice-Chancellor if he promised his support.

Hitler took a gamble and refused – he wanted to be Chancellor (prime minister). So Von Papen and Hindenburg gambled too and, on 30 January 1933 Hindenburg made Hitler Chancellor. He believed he could control Hitler; history would prove how mistaken he was. In the end, Hitler did not take power – he was given it.

Hitler visits Reich President Hindenburg and his grandchildren on his Neudeck estate.

Chapter 4

Propaganda

"It may be good to have power based on weapons…it is better and longer lasting, however, to win and hold the heart of a nation."

Joseph Goebbels, 1934

The following Nazi propaganda from 1945 claims that to give up and admit defeat would be worse than death for the German people. The two-page leaflet was designed to keep them fighting. The first page, outlined below, proves how strong and distinct the Nazi Propaganda actually was.

We are Germans!
There are two possibilities:
Either we are good Germans or we are bad ones.
If we are good Germans, all is well. If we are bad Germans,
Then there are two possibilities:
Either we believe in victory, or we do not believe in victory.
If we believe in victory, all is well. If we do not believe in victory,
Then there are two further possibilities:
Either we hang ourselves, or we do not hang ourselves. If we hang ourselves, all is well. If we do not hang ourselves,
Then there are two possibilities:
Either we give up the fight, or we do not give up the fight. If we do not give up, all is well. If we do give up,

Then there are again two possibilities:

Either the criminal Red mob following the Anglo-Americans liquidates us immediately, or following Stalin's wish, we are deported to work in the icy wastes of Siberia.

If we are liquidated immediately, that is comparatively speaking good. If they deport us to Siberia or somewhere else,

There are again two possibilities:

Either one dies during the march from the great stresses and privations, or one does not die immediately.

If one dies quickly, one has deserved it, but is still lucky. If one does not die quickly, that is unfortunate.

Once again, there are two possibilities:

Either one slaves away for foreigners until the end of his life, without ever seeing his homeland and his family again, or one gets a shot in the back of the neck a little earlier.

Since both of the last two possibilities end in death, there are no further possibilities.

Therefore:

There are not two possibilities!

There is only one!

We must win the war, and we can win it! Each man and each woman, the entire German people, must call forth their utmost in work, courage, and discipline.

Then our future and the future of our children will be assured, and the German people will be saved from a descent into Bolshevist chaos!

Source: Rüstzeug für die Propaganda in der Ortsgruppe, #2 (January 1945), p. 31

Material reproduced with the kind permission of Randall Bytwerk,

German Propaganda Archive: www.calvin.edu/academic/cas/gpa

Berliner! Schützt Euch und Eure Familie!

Meldet Euch zur Einwohnerwehr! Meldestellen: Für Berlin: Eden-Hotel, Garde-Kavallerie-Division, Abt. VIII. Friedenau: Königin-Luise-Gymn.-nasium, Goslarstr. 14. Schöneberg: Neues Rathaus, Zimmer 44. Steglitz: Rathaus, Dahlem: Podbielskiallee 78. Wilmersdorf: Schaperstr. 25. Charlottenburg: Rathaus, Zimmer 21. Lichterfelde: Drakestr., Gymnasium.

So what exactly was German propaganda and why did it exist? First, propaganda was central to the Nazi Party's persuasion of ordinary German people that war was essential and that they could, and would, win. It was important to convince the public to fight and that war was necessary. Second, it provided the party with the means by which to brow-beat an entire nation into believing what they were being told and it reasoned with them as to why they should tow the party line. German propaganda before and during the Second World War was extremely psychologically powerful. Having recently undergone a

Propaganda was not a new phenomenon. This 1919 *Freikorps* leaflet urged "Berliners! Protect yourselves and your families! Join the citizens' guard!

power struggle between the Nazi Party and the socialists, the former did not have enough power to enter, let alone incite a war. The early propaganda was designed to increase and fuel the wartime effort.

This came at a time when it was recognized across the party that Hitler and many of the high-ranking officials, fuelled by their own racism, were intent on seeing as many "inferior" races exterminated as possible. There was some unrest between German Jews and other Germans by the

An anti-Semitic
Nazi election
poster from 1924.

The message of this 1928 election poster for the Democratic Block was that "Those who wish to have justice, freedom, bread and happiness should vote for the parties of the Republic".

time the propaganda machine whirred into action, however, Hitler and his leaders knew that it would be necessary to convince the public of the need to be rid of their friends and neighbours. It was this anti-Semitic material that became the second agenda (after convincing the population that war was necessary) of Nazi propaganda.

Der Stürmer, the infamous newspaper, was responsible for much of the propaganda prior to the Second World War and for 22 years denounced the Jewish people on a weekly basis. Publisher Julius Streicher began the newspaper in 1923 in response to accusations that he was a liar and a coward. Attacks on the Jewish population began in the first issue published in May 1923 and continued unabated throughout the newspapers' shelf-life. With the

An NSDAP poster from 1932 raises the issue of unemployment and proclaims "Our last hope: Hitler".

assassination of leading Jewish politician, Walther Rathenau, and a venomous attack on the deceased in *Der Stürmer*, the paper became a weapon in the war against the Jews, although to begin with, the powers that were in the Nazi leadership were worried by Streicher's approach. In 1924, following a short lapse in publication, the paper became stronger than ever. Three years later and weekly circulation figures had grown to 14,000 copies. Another leading Jew, Mayor Luppe, had been the subject of most of the attacks during earlier issues, but once the paper's circulation had significantly increased, it became more of a German, rather than a Nuremberg publication and its coverage was steadily broadened. Material that was fresh and scandalous was a pre-requisite. Political scandals abounded during the early years. Jews were consistently blamed for German economic problems and then found themselves targeted in sensationalized journalism. Much of the scandal and filth brought the newspaper under attack itself. Jewish newspapers responded with complaints about how events were being sensationalized. Anonymous letters were submitted to other publications about the damning and truth-stretching stories that were portrayed in *Der Stürmer*. Many of the paper's readers were inexperienced adolescents craving for scandal and Streicher and his many staff were keen to provide it.

Much of the material came from Nazis and when there were no new scandals to report, revamped articles of old news became front page cover stories. Despite its criticism from many corners and initial concerns by the Nazi Party, *Der Stürmer* was eventually highly revered by Hitler. It appealed to the masses and was written specifically for this audience. It was powerful in its approach and captivated humble Germans (ironically many of them Jewish in its early days) and effectively became a paper of the people. Almost from the beginning, Streicher was aware that visual impact was just as important as words and he combined cartoons and photographs with simple, clear writing to manipulate and persuade the readership. It worked.

When Hitler was handed power in 1933, the paper was one of the best-selling Nazi publications in existence and leading Nazis, such as Max Amann, Robert Ley and Heinrich Himmler began promoting *Der Stürmer* alongside their own activities. When nine special editions were published to coincide with the Nuremburg rally, circulation often reached two million. The content remained the same; the crimes of the Jewish people. Showcases to promote the paper were positioned everywhere, including parks and streets and the publication became a part of everyday life. Hitler has been documented as reading every issue from start to finish. Success of the paper led Streicher to start publishing anti-Semitic books. The Gestapo were beginning to send in material for the paper about the criminal Jewish practices taking place throughout Germany. In fact, the paper had the authority to request whatever it wanted from the Gestapo and memos to officers were a regular occurrence outlining what they needed to provide for publication. With copies reaching South America and the United States, Streicher became a powerful major force in the destruction of the Jews.

But there were times when the paper pushed too far in its racial prejudices which resulted in international fury. However, Streicher would turn to Hitler for support and it

would be banned for a month or so at a time at most before being reinstated by the Nazi leader. As already mentioned, for twenty-two years *Der Stürmer* cited racial hatred and fear. During the latter war years, with most Jews either removed or annihilated, the German readership lost interest in the stories and Streicher was forced to change

Adolf Hitler is portrayed as a knight saving the German people in the mid-1930s.

This 1937 poster depicted the Nazi's view of "The Eternal Jew".

his tack and make the paper more focused on international issues. The final issue was published early in 1945 for a limited audience that had fallen to fewer than 200,000; it advocated that the invading Allies supported the Jewish conspiracy. Streicher would become a hero for later twentieth century anti-Semitic organizations and *Der Stürmer* was published during the 1970s – once again as a weapon – in the propaganda war of the modern-day world.

Audiences of the Nazi propaganda machine, prior to the Second World War, consisted of the German population who were constantly bombarded with information about the struggle of the Nazi Party and the fact that Germany needed to stand up to, and indeed fight, its foreign enemies – particularly the Jewish population. Even Germans living in other countries, including Poland, the Soviet Union, and France, in particular, were reminded of their allegiance to Germany. The power behind most of the propaganda alluded to the superiority and greatness of German military, cultural and scientific achievements. Prior to the Second World War, Joseph Goebbels was responsible, along with Streicher, for much of the early propaganda.

The German Minister for Public Enlightenment & Propaganda played a large part in the creation of pro-Nazi and anti-Semitic material for the Nazi Party. He cleverly devised a propaganda machine that saw instructions and

Joseph Goebbels at the opening of the radio and television show on 28 August 1936.

information sent out from party headquarters to local branches adapted and modified to suit a particular audience. All propaganda prior to 1943, when the Red Army finally defeated the German Army in Stalingrad on 4 February that year, had been designed to emphasize the greatness and political prowess of the German army and its humanitarian soldiers. Although this was far from the case, the German people lapped up the material devised

The message here was "Kids, what do you know about the Führer?"

by Goebbels and his ministry and believed that people in occupied territories were being treated fairly and decently by their own armed forces. Further information cited Allied pilots, who were bombing German cities, as murderous cowards while the American forces were likened to Al Capone. In an attempt to upset the Allied forces and separate the British and American troops from each other and both from the Red Army in the Soviet Union, more propaganda was infiltrated into all three sides.

Many different forms of propaganda were used. The newly invented radio became a huge cog in the propaganda machine. Speeches were also a vital part of getting information across. As with the notorious *Der Stürmer*, Nazi propaganda also used visual aids to get the Party message across. These were also of vital importance and did much to persuade people to toe the Party line. One of the most important mainstays of this was the use of posters which were targeted at audiences in both Germany and occupied territories. A great deal of research was undertaken to find exactly the right images to manipulate and motivate target audiences. Posters of soldiers looking strong and composed were used for new recruits to the army. Pictures of Adolf Hitler with simple slogans were designed to show a united, stable Germany that required the commitment and support of its people. Softer images of women and children were also used to capture the imaginations of the German people. They were created to show that despite war, the nation needed to unite and effectively pull together to make sure that Germany became a world superpower under the Nazi regime. Other nationals, including the Dutch were propositioned by

Adolf Hitler with
members of the
Hitler Youth at his
holiday residence
of Haus
Wachenfeld on
Obersalzberg near
Berchtesgaden.

posters asking them to join the German army. Mothers were incited to "fight" for their children and the Hitler Youth movement was born with the advent of posters inviting them to become new recruits in the search for truth and honour. War was depicted as an exciting opportunity where a plea to join the military was fashioned within the material. Once war got underway, posters advocating heavy production were prevalent. The use of mechanized tanks, which were vital to Hitler's army in their droves, required a great deal more industrialized production than Germany was used to. The significance of production and labour became a necessary reality and there was a real push by the Nazi leadership for increased productivity. Workers in Germany were encouraged to "do their bit" for the war effort. Posters designed to ram the message home often displayed muscular men hard at work as this strength was thought to inspire confidence. Known as production or labour propaganda, it became a huge chunk of the propaganda effort during the Second World War.

Running alongside the production propaganda was the campaign to conserve basic materials for the war effort. Although Germany didn't establish its own war efforts on home soil as early as the Allied nations, particularly the British, there were attempts to encourage the conservation of items and materials that were becoming increasingly scarce. Paper was one such commodity that was heavily championed and the public were once again invited to give to the war effort. Many of these posters depicted soldiers and soldiers in battle, however, others showed cheery Germans happily giving to the war effort. Whether the posters were battle clad or presenting cheery, smiling

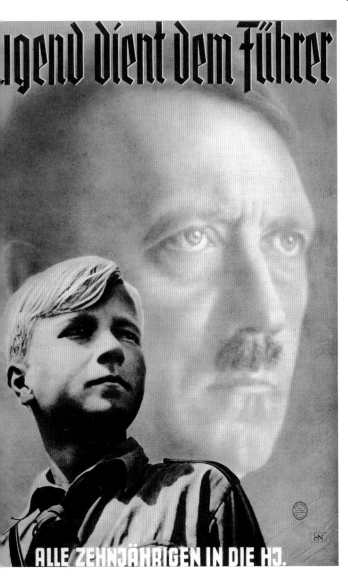

Igend dient dem Führer

ALLE ZEHNJÄHRIGEN IN DIE HJ.

"Youth serves the Führer! All ten-year-olds into the Hitler Youth." A 1935 poster.

faces, all of them glorified war. But many Germans were reluctant to give up their fast-disappearing luxuries

The poster for the Nazis' 1937 convention in Nuremberg.

despite the prevalence of "conservation posters" nationwide. Equally important were the propaganda posters which warned citizens that spies may be listening into conversations. However, these types of posters were few and far between during the war years. Average Germans were considered to know very little about the actual movements of troops or military plans, but "spying propaganda" would have helped mould the population into believing that loose talk and gossip could be overheard and would have brought about some realization that the war was very real on a basic, localized level. These posters also helped dissuade people from having their own conversations. Opinions were kept within small communities and, as long as people felt threatened, they were more likely to follow the demands of the government and adhere to Nazi propaganda in that threats and fear from the enemy would hopefully be eradicated. Posters in propaganda were also used to advertise other mediums such as films. The movie, "The Eternal Jew" was filmed to de-humanize the German Jews and openly compares the Jewish community to rats. Cheating over money was also widely advertised as a Jewish crime. With other prolific posters advocating that Hitler was a heroic, almost mythical man and the absolute head of the government, it was fairly easy to persuade the German population that they were indeed a chosen race and special people. It also helped to enhance national pride. With the likes of Goebbels glorifying the Führer in speeches and radio broadcasts, it was impossible for Germany as a nation to ignore the importance of the "task" that lay ahead for their country. The Third Reich was beginning to take a firm grasp of its own people. Communities were beginning to believe the hype and information that was coming their way and it was fast becoming apparent that the average German was strongly in support of the government and what Hitler was aiming to achieve.

In addition to the posters, another visual aid in the propaganda machine was the increasing use of cartoons and humour to depict stereotypes and pure prejudice. It was a useful, and effective, way of communicating and spreading racial hatred. It was designed to make Germans wary of their Jewish friends and neighbours and, once again, this ploy worked.

Also published, both by Nazis and their sympathizers, were a great number of books. Books which outlined ideals of anti-Semitism, German nationalism and eugenics had actually been published during the 1800s. The Third Reich were keen to embody these books with their strong ideals in their own publications. Hitler's book, *Mein Kampf* was based heavily on the ideals of *The Crowd: A Study of the Popular Mind* published in 1895 and written by Gustave Le Bon, a book which discusses the use of propaganda as a rational means by which to control the irrational behaviour of the "crowd" or population. Books by leading thinkers which outlined the differences between German Nordic or Aryan people compared to supposed other, inferior races and "aliens" were used in German classrooms.

The *Reichsministerium für Volksaufklärung und Propaganda* or *Propagandaministerium* (The Reich Ministry for Popular Enlightenment and Propaganda) was set up almost as soon as the Nazi Party took power. It was dedicated to the ideology that Hitler and his leaders advocated for the German people and was organized to regulate society and culture. At its head was Joseph Goebbels who was responsible for ensuring that all press and culture was controlled and monitored. Based in the Leopold Palace in Berlin-Mitte, the ministry enforced the Nazi doctrine and was effective in its manipulation and control of public opinion.

It came into its own at the outbreak of the Second World War, having already established itself as a

Poster for a 1938 calendar of the Racial Politics Office of the NSDAP portrays the *Neues Volk* (A New People), the Nazis' "superior" race of Aryans.

formidably powerful ministry. The propaganda machine was well organized and expertly planned and became a powerful psychological tool for the Nazis. There were three main branches in the ministry which comprised The Ministry for Enlightenment and Propaganda, The Reich Culture Chamber and the Central Propaganda Office of the Nazi Party. No wonder then that it was the largest and most prominent of all the Nazi ministries, however, the

Culture Chamber was the arm with the most obvious purpose. It gave licences – or not – to all media including the press, radio broadcasting, literature, film and the arts as well as music. This ensured that all forms of culture were heavily influenced and regulated and all were clearly under the manipulation of the Nazi Party. Working with Dr Joseph Goebbels was Dr Werner Naumann who was a state secretary within the ministry. He later became head of the ministry when Goebbels was promoted to Reichkanzler. Naumann's most famous speech "Capitulate, Never!" came in March 1945 in Munich. It specifically mentions the National Socialist Werewolf Resistance Movement which was a clandestine force which would carry out attacks on occupying forces should the Nazis fail and their regime come to an end. It was a particularly partisan organization whose guerrilla attacks included arson, sabotage, assassination and snipers. Naumann was also head of the Gauleiter Circle.

Another prominent member of the ministry was Hans Fritzsche, a senior Nazi official. Fritzsche had served in the German army in 1917 before attending university and becoming a journalist. He quickly took up a career in radio where he worked for the government before becoming head of the wireless news service in 1932. He was eventually promoted to the news section at the ministry and as deputy to Alfred Berndt at the press division. Within six years, Fritzsche had become chief of the Home Press Division where he stayed for four years before Goebbels decided to take personal control as part of his own quest for greater authority and acknowledgement from the Führer. Fritzsche was one of the few Nazi officials to be acquitted at Nuremberg following his arrest by Soviet forces in May 1945. However, he was found guilty of other crimes shortly after the trials and served nine years in prison. On his release he died from cancer.

Goebbels himself was an egomaniac who ordered the burning of books by all Jewish or anti-Nazi authors. It was one of his first acts of anti-Semitism. He was prolific in his attacks on the Jewish population through his speeches and the Nazi propaganda that would follow the party's rise to power in 1933. His status as Minister would lead Goebbels

A 1941 poster encouraging youngsters to join the Waffen-SS once they reached the age of seventeen.

This Nazi shop in Vienna, pictured in 1939, sold training material.

to gain full control over all information distributed. But it was his power and fierce attacks on the Jews that led to the first riotous acts carried out by the German army between 9 and 10 November 1938 that brought him notoriety. Known as *Kristallnacht*, or the Night of Broken Glass, the German army ransacked the homes of Jews in numerous cities across the country and also raided around 8,000 Jewish shops and businesses. Many Jews were beaten to death in the confusion that blanketed the atrocity while about 30,000 Jewish men were removed from their destroyed homes and ferried to concentration camps. The treatment of these men was particularly brutal, although most were allowed to leave after three months or so, providing they agreed to leave Germany for good. More than 260 synagogues were burned to the ground on *Kristallnacht*.

Goebbels was an avid supporter of war and to gain more power and prominence he was instrumental in using his relationships with German officers to propel himself ever upward within the party which sometimes resulted in him switching alliances. Despite the defeat of the Sixth Army at Stalingrad, and realization that the Axis powers were facing an inevitable defeat, Goebbels continued to use his well-oiled propaganda machine to convince the German people that the only option available to them was to continue with the war. There was no going back. There would be no defeat. Although in 1926 Goebbels had been disillusioned with Hitler's vision which he thought reactionary, he was spurred on by his leader's interest in him.

Hitler had been shrewd enough to know that Goebbel's craved recognition and the Führer would not disappoint. At a private audience with Hitler, Goebbels voiced his unstinting support for Hitler, and his ideology, which would prove to be a firm declaration that he would follow to the end of his life. As a result Goebbels became party leader for the Berlin National Socialists where he discovered his talents as a propagandist. It also afforded the egotist the opportunity to satisfy his thirst for violence in the street fights he ordered where he challenged opposition parties. Using SA stormtroopers he deliberately provoked, chastized and created havoc and mayhem. He put fear on a very real level while continuing to edit the Nazi newspaper, *Der Angriff* in Berlin. He became widely feared in Berlin as he frequently targeted Jews, particularly religious leaders and politicians. His part in bringing the Nazis to power earned him his ministerial post and a seat in the Cabinet.

His sarcastic "humour" in which he delighted in his speeches did little to conceal the very real threat that was inevitably facing the Jewish population and he managed through his appointment as Gauleiter of Berlin to put pressure on the Jewish community by forcing them out of their businesses. He also banned Jews from using public transport and other city facilities, and in any way that he could, Goebbels would deliberately put obstacles in the way of Jewish citizens just trying to go about their everyday lives. It was Goebbels in mid-1938 who investigated whether it would be possible to devise a mark that all Jewish people should wear to identify the fact that they were Jewish. He was desperate to get them out of Germany – in fact, he wanted them out of Europe altogether. He also wanted to instigate a ghetto where all Jewish members of society would have to live (until he could push them out of Germany and Europe). He didn't manage to get what he wanted at that time – but these ideas would all too soon become a reality under a government fuelled by hatred and racial prejudice.

While working on his plans for the Jewish community and devising its downfall, Goebbels was also busy preparing Germany for war. He was intent on making the German people see that war was necessary and above all he wanted them to welcome and applaud it. But he was wise enough to know that the majority of Germans did not want to go to war so he used his propaganda at a crucial time to persuade and manipulate. He was the first to direct the campaign against Poland and fabricated stories with regard to Germans in cities throughout the country in order to convince his homeland that war would put an end to any threat the Polish people might pose. With war underway, Goebbels needed to change his tack and he became the face and voice of the Nazi Party in domestic issues while Nazi officials were preoccupied with Germany's fighting forces. Having total control over what was filtered to the masses, The Ministry for Enlightenment and Propaganda cleverly devised and disseminated propaganda which would prove to be an all important weapon against the Jewish population (and even the German population), and would lead to wartime atrocities, the like of which had never been seen before. It also served to provide the stepping stones the Nazis needed to secure their grip across Europe, and beyond, in their quest for supremacy .

It wasn't long before Goebbels had his wish of identifying all Jews. This picture shows a boy in the Warsaw Ghetto in 1940 selling the Star of David armbands that Jews were forced to wear.

Chapter 5

The seizure and consolidation of power

The day on which Adolf Hitler became Chancellor of Germany, 30 January 1933, was an historic one. This seizure of power was later described as "The hour of the birth of the Third Reich". The third German Empire after the Holy Roman and Bismarckian was scheduled to last a thousand years but in the event only lasted twelve.

With a cabinet numerically dominated by conservatives, Hitler still had work to do, but by giving his two cabinet members, Hermann Goering and Wilhelm Flick, the key posts of Ministers of the Interior in Prussia and the Reich, he eased his task considerably. The country had been struggling for some while against the problems of the world economic depression with a minority government, and changes at the top had been rapid as Chancellor after Chancellor struggled in vain. Heinrich Brüning resigned in May 1932 to be replaced by Franz von Papen of the central Catholic BVP party, but again a minority government had resulted at the subsequent polls.

A second 1932 election in November failed to resolve things and the impotent von Papen had been replaced as Chancellor by General Kurt von Schleicher, but he resigned in January 1933 when President Hindenburg refused to let him continue to govern by presidential decree. Von Papen, who became vice-chancellor, persuaded Hindenburg to appoint Hitler, saying that he would be able to prevent him from introducing his more extremist policies.

The door opened for Hitler and the Nazi Party, and they took full advantage. But not everybody supported them, as became apparent when the Reichstag building, symbol of the German state and of democracy, was torched by an arsonist in late February. A Dutch communist, Marinus van der Lubbe, was found guilty, sentenced to death and beheaded (the customary German execution method at the time) in January 1934, but some suggested the Nazis had been involved themselves so they could step up persecution of the Communists and reap political

Hitler's first Cabinet after his appointment as Reich Chancellor, 30 January 1933. Front row (l-r) Hermann Goering, Adolf Hitler, Franz von Papen; back row (l-r) Franz Seldte, Gericke, Johann Graf Schwerin von Krosigk, Wilhelm Frick, Werner von Blomberg and Alfred Hugenberg.

benefit. At any event the Reichstag Fire Decree was issued, and civil liberties suspended.

In retrospect, the Reichstag fire was the point from which Nazi Germany became a centrally controlled totalitarian regime thanks to new laws giving Hitler unlimited power. Over the next five months, the Nazis systematically caused all opposition political parties to shut down in a process known as *Gleichschaltung* ("co-ordination"). At the beginning of June Hitler increased the number of Nazis in his government, and by the middle of July was insisting the Nazi Party was "the only political party in Germany."

By the end of July 1933, it was estimated there were nearly 27,000 people being held in protective custody merely for holding opposing views to the ruling Nazis. They were housed in abandoned army and police barracks, the predecessors of the dreaded concentration camps. The first of these was established at Dachau in March 1933. And because many dissidents were Jews, this was to be a place from which they would never emerge.

Hitler's first move on becoming Chancellor was to call an election, the third within the space of a year, to legitimize and if possible extend his power. This took place in March 1933 and saw the Nazi NSDAP win forty-four per cent of the popular vote. They had added over five and a half million votes to their total, but still lacked overall control without the assistance of the Nationalist DNVP party who had polled a small but significant eight per cent.

Turnout for the election was 88.7 per cent, an astonishingly high figure that suggested Hitler's appeal to a disaffected nation was snowballing. (His own, cynical view on elections was summed up in *Mein Kampf*: "It is

The majority of the Reichstag building was destroyed by a fire started during the night of 27 February 1933.

SA and SS paramilitary units continue their reign of terror against Communists in Chemnitz in March 1933.

easier for a camel to pass through the eye of a needle than for a great man to be discovered by an election.")

The task of winning the election had been assisted by a decree giving the state the power to ban public meetings and gag the press if it was considered to pose a threat to national security. Such blanket bans were ruthlessly exploited to stamp out opposition. The German Communist Party (KPD) overnight became an illegal organization and the state police arrested nearly 100

communist Reichstag deputies, the leader of whom, Ernst Torgler, had voluntarily surrendered himself to the police. After, the remainder was forced into hiding as the Nazis had a majority on their own.

The press, along with the arts, radio and films, was tightly controlled by Joseph Goebbels. He ensured that newspapers which dared to criticize the Nazis were closed down, while those which survived took their news from the Nazi news agency DNB. A book-burning, presided

Radio was not Hitler's only method of getting his message across. Here a teacher gives a history lesson based heavily on the Nazi ideology announced by Reich Interior Minister Frick in his school reform programme of May 1933.

over by Goebbels in 1933, saw "un-German" tomes by Einstein, Freud, Herman Hesse and Erich Kästner set alight on public bonfires.

Hitler made good use of radio, the best pre-television medium to reach Germans in their homes. In his first year as Chancellor he made fifty radio broadcasts – and with German factories churning out cheap sets by the thousand, seventy per cent of families had one at the outbreak of war. The favoured waveband was short range, which meant Germans could not hear differing versions of the news from foreign stations, only Nazi propaganda. Tuning in to foreign stations during wartime would be a treasonable offence.

Hitler wanted to dismantle the system of local government and replace it with central control. He achieved this by having the Nazi Party's competing paramilitary wings, the brown-shirted *Sturm Abteilung* and SS (*Schutzstaffel*), formed in 1925 as Hitler's personal bodyguards, cause unrest thereby allowing the imposition of Nazi Reich commissioners to restore order.

The SA and SS targeted the *Länder* (or districts) where the NSDAP did not have control. These included Bavaria, Baden, Hesse, Saxony and Würtemburg, as well as the city states of Bremen, Hamburg and Lübeck. Bavaria put up the strongest resistance, but as the Reichstag Fire Decree had given the Reich government carte blanche to overrule the individual *Länder* governments, President Hindenburg was able to ignore their appeals. In 1934, state governments were abolished altogether and for the next eleven years Germany would be ruled firmly and forcefully from the centre.

Sepp Dietrich, leader of the SS Group East, in conversation with brigade leader Henze during the inspection of SS Group East at the Tempelhofer Feld (centre, Group Squadron Leader Stein).

Nazi party support was traditionally high in the rural areas, since workers in the cities often preferred to stay loyal to their unions. Farmers were having a hard time of it, especially since agricultural prices had stayed low after the raging hyperinflation of the 1920s, and they were keen to give the Nazis a try. Some of the middle class also feared a communist revolution, which would give the working class the privileges they traditionally enjoyed, so also supported the Nazis.

The *Sturm Abteilung* glorified violence and used its privileged position to assault opponents and vandalize the property of those who had displeased it. This included the political left and the Catholic Church. The SA was also at the forefront of enforcing a short-lived national boycott of Jewish businesses in April 1933.

The boycott of Jewish shops came into force on 1 April 1933.

A new police force was created which would further encourage a climate of fear under Hitler. The *Geheime Staatspolizei*, a new department of the Prussian state police

Loading confiscated books onto a truck to be taken to the book burning at Berlin's Opernplatz on 10 May 1933.

affiliated with the Ministry of the Interior, would become better known by its abbreviated title, the Gestapo. Its job was to eliminate by any means necessary all opposition to the Nazis within Germany and its occupied territories. Hermann Goering, Prussian Minister of the Interior, took command in April 1933 of a force whose actions were not subject to judicial appeal.

The Gestapo could arrest anyone and send them to a concentration camp without trial. They used informers to uncover covert attempts at opposition and their calculating methods made them the model for secret police services that followed in totalitarian states. And though the Gestapo's victims did not have recourse to the courts to save them, Hitler's creation of the People's Court in 1934

Parade of the SA
and SS during the
NSDAP's Party
Convention of
Victory in
September 1933.

SA and SS troops march in to intimidate the opposition in the second session of the new Reichstag on 23 March 1933 for the vote on the "Law for the Removal of the Distress of People and Reich" – the so called Enabling Act.

to try "enemies of the state" ensured all opponents of the Nazis had no hope of justice. By 1939 the People's Court had sent 500 to their death and many more to concentration camps.

The passage of the Enabling Act in late March 1933 granted full legislative powers to the Chancellor without requiring the assent of the Reichstag. Passed with the aid of the Centre Party and in the absence of the Communist deputies, it would be the formal basis of Hitler's power for the remainder of the Third Reich. While it was surprising that the Centre Party would agree to this, the country had been ruled by presidential decree for the previous three years, so the difference maybe did not seem that great.

Hitler was keen to keep Jews squarely in his sights as scapegoats for any problems that might arise. Although Jews in 1933 made up only one per cent of the German population, they also accounted for ten per cent of lawyers and sixteen per cent of doctors, so it was not hard to see how Germans could be jealous of their success, as well as being suspicious of their different religion. The dismissal of all Jews from the civil service via the Law for the Restoration of the Professional Civil Service proved effective.

The Communists were hardly faring better: half of the 300,000 Germans who were members of the KPD in January 1933 would end up in concentration camps, and

One of the first things Hitler did after coming to power was to order the reconstruction of the German Navy and Air Force.

30,000 would die there. The trade unions remained the one last possible obstacle to Hitler's plans, so in May 1933 he declared that all of these would be absorbed into a single union, the *Deutsche Arbeitsfront* (DAF). He sold the idea to the workers by explaining it would have increased bargaining power against employers, but in reality it had nothing of the kind. Indeed strikes would soon be made illegal.

The Treaty of Versailles had attempted, feebly, to prevent Germany from re-arming. Hence in 1932 the fraction of the country's national product spent on armament and defence had been a mere one per cent. This would rise to nearly twenty-five per cent by the end of the decade as war approached.

A clause in the Treaty of Versailles allowed Germany to build ships up to 10,000 tons with guns of up to 11 inches diameter; these were classed as coast-defence battleships. The pocket battleship *Deutschland* was one of three such ships whose construction began between 1928 and 1931 and was completed in April 1933. The shipbuilders pushed

the envelope at Hitler's request, so Germany had to under-report the vessel's weight to avoid violating the treaty. The British and French were at the time unconcerned about the class of ship, as they had individual vessels that were superior – typical of the complacent attitude that would make Hitler's task of re-armament so much easier.

At the end of May Hitler inspected the German fleet at Kiel and met with leading SS and government officials including General von Blomberg, Admiral Raeder, Goering and von Papen on board the *Leipzig*. October would see Germany withdraw from both the Disarmament Conference and the League of Nations, actions approved by over ninety per cent of voters in a year-end referendum.

Later in the year Hitler would step up the preparation of a clandestine Luftwaffe (Air Force), pilots for which had henceforth been trained at the Lipezk Airfield in Russia under a secret deal with the Red Army. The *Deutscher Luftsport-Verband*, an organization for "air-minded young men", would be given its own uniform with rank and trade insignia. The secret school at Lipezk was abandoned, as was any real pretence, as the DLV trained its members in the aeronautical skills of ballooning, gliding and powered flight. (The Treaty of Versailles specifically forbade Germany to have an air force.)

Lufthansa, Germany's airline, had long been in the forefront of civil aviation, and this too would feed personnel and expertise into the nascent Luftwaffe. The state airline was subsidized to the tune of 50 per cent, Hitler being mindful of its use in war. By 1939 the Luftwaffe would have over 8,000 aircraft, with many Lufthansa airframes also available to it as a welcome bonus.

But it wasn't only the military that would benefit from Hitler's aspirations. June brought the implementation of the Reinhardt Plan, which comprised increased expenditure on public works made possible by Germany's failure to pay reparations to the war victors. Most notable of these projects was the construction of highways known as autobahns. One reason for this was to absorb some of the six million unemployed, and by 1935 the scheme was already employing some 350,000 people. The system survives to this day as one of the most obvious, lasting reminders of Nazi rule.

Another beneficiary would be the car industry. Hitler had a keen interest in cars even though he did not drive himself and, in 1933, he asked Ferdinand Porsche to make changes to an original 1931 design to make it more suited for the working man. This would emerge a few years later as the Volkswagen or "people's car".

Perhaps surprisingly, Hitler was also concerned at this time to make peace with the Vatican. This was partly to nullify the Centre Party which the Vatican had hitherto supported. Pope Pius XI agreed a concordat that gave Germans the right to practise religion and allowed the church independence, with the proviso that Catholic priests were not to involve themselves in politics. Negotiated by the Catholic Franz von Papen, it gave the Nazi regime certain legitimacy. Typically, violations by Germany began almost immediately.

Ferdinand Porsche would later give Hitler one of his Beetles as a birthday present.

Ernst Röhm with
Hitler in 1933.

But there was an enemy within for him to quell. The increasing power of the now nearly three million strong SA under its ambitious leader Ernst Röhm represented a threat to Hitler's dictatorship, and both Goering and Himmler advised him he would be safer to trust the top officials of the army and navy. The year of 1933, Hitler's first in power, ended with the ceremonial consecration of the *Leibstandarte* SS, Hitler's Praetorian Guard. Though Himmler commanded the unit, which functioned within the SS organization, its members swore a personal oath of allegiance to the Führer, not to Germany – a sign of things to come.

As the year of 1934 dawned, Hitler began a display of seemingly peaceful intent by signing a non-aggression treaty with neighbouring Poland; this also served to make France's policy of defensive alliances against Germany appear risible. Just two months later, however, he was to announce an increase in the size of the German Army.

The end was nigh for *Sturm Abteilung* leader Ernst Röhm, who had given a speech in which he claimed that the SA was the true army of National Socialism and that the regular army should be relegated to a training organization. He finally paid the price for his ambition in June. Hitler could not afford to alienate the army or the conservatives who were backing him, so decided to eradicate the SA threat. He was encouraged in this by Heinrich Himmler, leader of the rival SS, who believed the SA were about to seize power, while the army, who were mostly First World War veterans, were fearful of being taken over by the SA. Hitler was particularly keen to keep them on his side.

On 11 April in a pact made on board the *Deutschland* warship, Hitler persuaded the top officials of the army and navy to back his bid to succeed Hindenburg as president,

Hindenburg greets Hitler in front of the Neue Wache in Berlin on what had been *Volkstrauertag* (Memorial Day), celebrated as *Heldengedenktag* (Remembrance Day) for the first time in February 1934.

by promising to "diminish" the three-million-strong SA and greatly expand the regular army and navy. When, five weeks later, the German officer corps endorsed Hitler to succeed the ailing President Hindenburg, the writing was on the wall for Röhm and his *Sturm Abteilung*.

The action at the Bavarian resort of Bad Wiessee in which Hitler had the senior leadership of the SA assassinated in late June 1934 came to be known as the Night of the Long Knives. Over the next few days, at least eighty-five people lost their lives in an indiscriminate killing spree, the victims including politicians like Kurt von Schleicher, Hitler's immediate predecessor as Chancellor, who was not a Nazi let alone a member of the SS. The final death toll may have been in the hundreds, and more than a thousand of Hitler's opponents were arrested.

Other peripheral figures to lose their lives included Gregor Strasser, leader of the NSDAP's left wing, conservative publicist Edgar Jung and Gustav von Kahr, Bavarian Premier at the time of the Beer Hall *putsch* of 1923. As it turned out Röhm, the main target, survived the *putsch* and was held briefly at Stadelheim Prison in Munich, while Hitler considered his fate. He was eventually shot at point-blank range in his cell when he refused to commit suicide.

Defending the purge, Hitler declared that to defend Germany he had the right to act unilaterally without resort to the courts. He was clearly prepared to answer to no-one. His speech to the Reichstag was broadcast to the nation and included the following: "In this hour I was responsible for the fate of the German people, and thereby I became the supreme judge of the German people. I gave the order

Rudolf Hoess enters the Kroll-Oper building prior to Hitler's government announcement to the Reichstag on 13 July 1934 concerning the "Night of the Long Knives" (30 June 1934).

to shoot the ringleaders in this treason, and I further gave the order to cauterise down to the raw flesh the ulcers of this poisoning of the wells in our domestic life. Let the nation know that its existence – which depends on its internal order and security – cannot be threatened with impunity by anyone! And let it be known for all time to come that if anyone raises his hand to strike the State, then certain death is his lot."

The Cabinet announces the law on building up the Wehrmacht and introduction of compulsory military service on 16 March 1935.

Hitler named Victor Lutze to replace Röhm as head of the *Sturm Abteilung*, but he was weak and did little to assert the SA's independence in the coming years, with the result that the once-feared force plummeted from 2.9 million members in August 1934 to 1.2 million in April

1938. By contrast, the black-shirted *Schutzstaffel* (SS) grew ever stronger as its traditional rival waned. Its leader, Himmler, also controlled the Gestapo and was rapidly gathering powers for himself prior to becoming chief of police in 1936.

When the long-ailing President Hindenburg died in August, the only barrier between Adolf Hitler and unrestricted power disappeared. Hitler issued a decree appointing himself *Führer und Reichskanzler* (Leader and Chancellor). Though illegal, the German people overwhelmingly approved the merger of the offices in a poll. Hitler also became commander of the armed forces. Again, the army swore allegiance to their Führer, not their Fatherland. Hitler now had complete control and Germany became a dictatorship.

A Rally of Unity held in Nuremberg in September saw Hitler proclaim the advent of a Thousand Year Reich. It was recorded by film-maker Leni Riefenstahl, who made it into a three-hour film entitled *Triumph of the Will*. (Banned in America, the film won many international awards as a ground-breaking example of film-making and is widely regarded as one of the most effective pieces of propaganda ever produced.)

In order to provide the next generation, a thriving Hitler Youth organization now operated to control the out-of-school lives of German boys from the age of fourteen. The girls' version was the BDM or *Bund Deutscher Mädel*. By 1935, the strength of these organizations was an impressive 2.3 and 1.5 million respectively.

The year of 1935, the third of Hitler's reign, would see Germany make giant steps towards a war footing. When, on 16 March, he repudiated the disarmament clauses of the

Versailles Treaty, it was a clear sign of changing times. Hitler announced that Germany would introduce compulsory military service, thereby creating an army of thirty-six divisions. Germany also formally revealed the existence of the hitherto forbidden Luftwaffe.

Germany began to rearm openly, and the reintroduction of universal conscription proved popular. The treaty had limited the size of the German army to 100,000 men, but between 1933 and 1939 its size would expand twenty-fold, the number of active divisions rising from ten to fifty-one. The army would until 1938 retain its autonomy from the state.

In addition, Hitler seemed determined to reintegrate ethnic Germans living outside Germany into the Reich. His initial victory was a bloodless one, the Saar becoming part of Germany again after a plebiscite. More than ninety per cent wanted to be part of Hitler's success story despite trade union and Catholic resistance. Hitler's territorial annexation would become both more widespread and forceful later in the decade as he broadened the search for living space (*lebensraum*).

The Luftwaffe was officially formed in April, while the following month saw the German Navy, formerly the Reichsmarine, renamed the Kriegsmarine. (*Krieg* meaning war.) The first of a new class of submarine, U-1, was commissioned in June. The build-up of the arms industry, of course, had a welcome spin-off in mopping up unemployment. The industrialists, who were happy the socialist *Sturm Abteilung* had been nipped in the bud, were now fully behind Hitler.

Britain's response came that same month when a Naval Agreement with Germany was signed, signalling that the

Western powers would try to tame Hitler by "appeasement"' rather than confront the Nazi Party head-on. Admiral Erich Raeder, Commander-in-Chief of the German Navy, claimed that the Agreement ruled out the possibility of Germany ever having to fight another war against Britain.

Elsewhere in Europe, countries were frantically attempting to find strength and safety in numbers. In May 1935, France and the Soviet Union concluded negotiations for a five-year Treaty of Mutual Assistance, although the treaty was never ratified by France, while October saw Czechoslovakia and the Soviet Union sign a five-year Treaty of Mutual Assistance. Hitler, for his part, agreed not to intervene in Austrian affairs or attempt to add Austria to the German Reich.

He also voluntarily agreed to restrict German maritime strength to thirty-five per cent of that of the Royal Navy, but as submarines were considered as a separate case, a real ratio of forty-five per cent resulted. (Germany's U-boats, of course, would be the cutting edge of their wartime maritime threat.)

In May 1935, Germany joined Italy in a non-aggression pact with France and Britain. The other powers now clearly rated Germany as an equal, quietly sweeping such matters as Versailles and the League of Nations under the carpet. But the 1935 invasion of Abyssinia (Ethiopia), Italy's blatant attempt to become a major power in the Mediterranean, won German support, creating a link that would continue and indeed deepen in the years to come with the declaration in 1937 of the Rome-Berlin Axis.

The seventh Nazi Party Congress in September 1935 saw the Nazi swastika adopted as the official national flag.

More important, if less symbolic, was the introduction of a new Reich Citizen's Law, and a Law for the Protection of German Blood and German Honour. These so-called Nuremberg Laws introduced two levels of citizenship, the *Reichbürger*, a Citizen of Pure German Blood, and a *Staatsangehörige*, a subject of the state – in other words, a Jew. (Gypsies, already unpopular pre-Hitler, were also classed as aliens and were equally subject to the Nuremberg laws.)

Intermarriage or even sexual intercourse between the groups was forbidden, while Jews, not being full German citizens, could not vote. "Jewishness" was defined by one's grandparents; having even one Jewish grandparent was sufficient to be deemed Jewish. With these factors exacerbated by the education system, which encouraged "pure" Germans to shun Jews, it is little wonder that the five years from 1933 saw thirty per cent of Germany's Jews leave the country for good.

Hitler's foreign policy had added to the German Reich without spilling a drop of German blood. The re-arming of Germany had created a feel-good factor among its citizens who had been leaderless for so long, endured hyperinflation and unemployment, and even seen foreign troops set foot on their soil when French and Belgian troops invaded the Ruhr in 1923 in protest at delayed payment of the war debt.

By the summer of 1935, Germany's unemployed who had numbered six million in the winter of 1932 had been slashed to 1.7 million. Germany was once again being regarded as a force in the world and was no longer the post-Versailles whipping boy. The next few years leading up to war would see Hitler build on this success.

Chapter 6

The road to war

Under the conditions set out in the Treaty of Versailles, the Rhineland was a demilitarized zone into which Germany was not allowed to take its troops, despite having some political control in the area. Even though the Rhineland was in Germany itself, without full control over it, many Germans felt that they had little say in what happened there.

Hitler decided to take a huge gamble in March 1936 when he ordered that German troops should reoccupy the Rhineland, blatantly defying the conditions set out in the treaty. The only worry that Hitler foresaw was what the French would make of the situation, and more importantly, what they would do about it. He ordered his

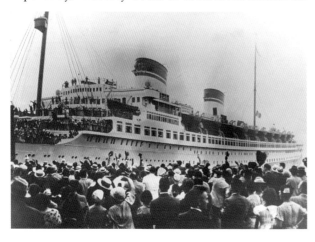

The Nuremberg race laws of September 1935 saw Jews emigrating from Germany en masse.

military high command that should France stand up to German troops then they were to make a hasty retreat. More than 32,000 soldiers and armed police crossed the border and into the Rhineland. France was not really in a position to challenge the Nazi leader. The country was in political turmoil and was hampered by its lack of strong leadership in government. In addition, Britain saw the reoccupation as troops simply entering their own "back

German troops enter the demilitarised Rhineland in March 1936 in breach of the Treaty of Versailles.

yard". The British also didn't feel that the conditions set out in the treaty needed to be enforced at this time and the general view taken by both the French and the British was that Germany was behaving understandably and reasonably.

No action was taken against the Nazi regime which must have come as a huge relief to Hitler who later commented that the reoccupation of the Rhineland had indeed been a nerve-racking experience. The inaction of both countries showed Hitler that when he did ignore terms of treaties he was able to carry out his plans with little or no interference from those who might have challenged him. In addition, the French had completely overlooked the fact that by choosing to do nothing over Hitler's actions they had made themselves vulnerable. The treaty had been signed by the French to protect themselves from an invading German army, following the First World War.

The Rhineland was supposed to act as their barrier against the Germans should they need it. They had considerably larger and stronger forces than the Germans, but the British government's insistence to keep on negotiating at all costs, meant that France didn't have the aptitude to challenge their neighbours. At this point it looked as if they had absolutely no interest in fighting for their own safety.

Hitler, strengthened by events, turned his attention to the east of Europe where France was even less likely to become involved. He was also supported in the media who believed that some elements of the treaty were simply not appropriate to 1930s Europe. The reason that Hitler gave for reoccupying the Rhineland was simple; the pact, for mutual assistance, that had been made between France and the Soviet Union in February 1936 could be seen as a direct threat against Germany. Although Germany was supposedly unable to build a naval force following the First World War, the British, in fact, signed their own pact with Germany in 1936 allowing the Führer the opportunity to put together a battle fleet which would include submarines. The Germans were not the only ones violating the conditions of the treaty. Reactions from countries which had signed the treaty were mixed, but none offered to do anything about German troops in the Rhineland. When the Council of the League of Nations finally met to discuss the event in London, the only objection to the reoccupation came from Maxim Litvinov of the Soviet Union. It was agreed that Hitler had blatantly breached the treaties of Versailles and Locarno, but he was, nevertheless, invited to plan a new scheme for Europe's safety whereupon he claimed that he had "no territorial claims in Europe". He also stated he wanted a twenty-five-year pact of non-aggression with the British and the French. The British tried to follow up on this declaration by the Führer but, interestingly, they never received a reply.

Joachim von Ribbentrop, Ambassador Extraordinary, with his delegation in London where he sought to justify the entry of German troops into the Rhineland before the Council of the League of Nations.

German Heinkel bombers on an airfield in Spain in 1936 during the Spanish Civil War.

Four months later and Hitler's route to having the war he dreamed of was helped by the major conflict that broke out in Spain following years of escalating internal tensions. The Spanish Civil War began in July 1936 when the coup organized by some members of the army tried to overthrow the government of the Second Spanish Republic. The results of the conflict were devastating and helped to increase tensions leading up to the outbreak of the Second World War. It has been described subsequently as a world war by proxy and Germany, in particular, used the civil war as a rehearsal for many *blitzkrieg* tactics it was to use in Hitler's quest for dominance after 1939. The Spanish Civil War became most notable for the political division that it created and for the atrocities that both sides committed.

In April 1939, the rebels won their fight and war came to an end with the installation of the dictator, Nationalist General, Francisco Franco. Those who helped to bring Franco to power included the Axis powers of Fascist Italy and, of course, Nazi Germany along with support from Portugal. The Soviet Union and Mexico had been on the opposing side supporting the Republic. In fact, the civil war had gained the interest of many non-Spanish citizens who participated in combat as well as advisory positions. Foreign governments had provided a large amount of financial assistance and military aid to Franco's forces. Both Hitler and Mussolini sent troops, aircraft, tanks and other weapons to support Franco. *Corpo Truppe Volontarie* (Volunteer Troops) arrived from Italy while Germany provided the Condor Legion. Overall around 95,000 Germans and Italians fought in Spain. Interestingly, Spain

Hitler climbs the speaker's stand at the 1937 Harvest Day celebration in Bückeberg.

had become a focus for pacifist organizations during the early 1930s including the War Resisters' International the president of which was Labour Party Leader, George Lansbury. The prominent Spanish pacifist, José Brocca made the argument that the Spanish pacifists had little choice but to make a stand against fascism. Brocca was instrumental in organizing agricultural workers to maintain food supplies and arranged humanitarian aid to war refugees throughout the civil war.

Atrocities on both sides were common and became the forerunners to those events carried out in the Second World War. Cities were bombed from the air and the execution of school teachers, for their beliefs in anti-clerical laicism, became commonplace. Genocide was carried out in the cities that were taken by the fascists and all those who were known to have Republican sympathies were executed alongside trade unionists. Catholics, on the other hand became the target for Republican supporters. More than 7,000 bishops, priests, other religious leaders and nuns were killed. Some were thrown down mine shafts,

Soldiers practise the goose-step that has become synonymous with the Nazis.

others forced to dig their own graves before being buried alive. Some died from being forced to swallow their own rosary beads.

Back in Germany, Hitler had decided that military conscription (lasting two years) would once again be enforced. It would again be another blatant act of defiance against the Treaty of Versailles as by making enrolment in the army compulsory, the Führer was effectively increasing the army to 550,000 men. The German High Command was nervous. Some generals thought that following the reoccupation of the Rhineland and the country's involvement in the Spanish Civil War Germany could be facing an immediate military attack, but apart from a few diplomatic protests, absolutely nothing else happened. It just strengthened Hitler's resolve further and his second gamble against his old enemies, the British and the French, had paid off. With the political crises still

Adolf Hitler arrives at an observation point as the German Army conducts manoeuvres in Mecklenburg.

Members of the
Hitler Youth
accompany the
Führer at
Thanksgiving Day
celebrations in
1937.

ongoing in France and Britain in the grip of economic depression Hitler had counted on both countries having enough problems to worry about without being too perturbed at his plans to build up his army. His shrewd thinking had paid dividends.

The Hitler Youth (in German, *Hitler-Jugend*) worked alongside the regular army as a paramilitary organization which was founded one year after the SA (*Sturm Abteilung*) in 1922. The idea, was that all young recruits would be trained, and eventually serve as future members of the SA within the Nazi Party. The movement was essentially disbanded in 1923 – although some still operated clandestine groups – until it was formally re-established in 1926 and reorganized by Kurt Gruber and this time became an integral part of the SA. More than 25,000 boys aged from fourteen years upwards were recruited by 1930. There was also a group for boys aged ten to fourteen and a girls group for those aged ten to eighteen was also established. Although banned briefly in 1933 by Heinrich Bruning, the Hitler Youth was brought back to action by the Chancellor's successor, Franz von Papen, who wanted to appease Hitler while his political career was flourishing. An expansion drive also started that same year and a Reich Youth Leader (*Reichsjugendfuhrer*) was installed when Baldur von Schirach took over the newly created post.

As part of the larger Nazi plan, the Hitler Youth were seen as the future "Aryan supermen" who were indoctrinated with anti-Semitism. They had instilled in them the motivation that would enable them in later life to

It was not just the next male generation of Germany that was being groomed to adore Hitler. Here the Führer meets members of the BDM ("League of German Maidens").

become faithful soldiers for the Third Reich. The emphasis was strongly on military training. When the scout movement was banned in German-controlled territories and countries the Hitler Youth took over many of the same activities although these were clearly changed in their content and their overall intention.

From 1936, membership of the Hitler Youth became compulsory and it was seen as an important stepping stone to membership of the SS. The movement was

Adolf Hitler and the Italian dictator, Benito Mussolini.

organized into local cells at community level and weekly meetings were held where Nazi doctrines were taught.

Elsewhere, Mussolini announced from the cathedral in Milan on 1 November 1936 that Italy and Germany had formed the Rome–Berlin Axis. The alliance had been developed over some time but this was the first time that the word Axis had been used. Italy, it was announced, would stand with Germany in the event of war. Prior to the Rome–Berlin Axis, although in agreement over many issues, Mussolini and Hitler had been mistrusting of each other and no formal agreement had ever been reached. However, after Italy had invaded Ethiopia (Abyssinia) and severed its ties to the democratic states, it was ready for an alliance with Nazi Germany. It was this very event that set the stage for the Second World War. The countries that would be on opposing sides were beginning to become clear and when the tensions between Italy and Britain in the Mediterranean became too much it was this, combined with Hitler's invasion of Poland that would lead to the outbreak of the longest and worst war ever seen. Knowing that they now had a solid ally, both Italy and Germany were confident that victory would be theirs should war eventually be declared. The Axis then cemented their alliance some three years later with the Pact of Steel in May 1939.

Following on from the Rome–Berlin Axis, Germany then made the Anti-Comintern Pact with Japan later that same month. It was directed primarily against the Soviet Union as part of the Communist International (Comintern). Should the Soviet Union attack either country then the two countries agreed to consult on safeguarding their common interests. Both agreed to never

make any political treaties with the Soviet Union and Germany also agreed to recognize Manchukuo. By this time, the Four Year Plan had been underway for some time. The Nazi Party wanted to create a series of economic reforms to ensure the protection of agriculture and economic independence. Also part of the plan was to increase production of synthetic fibre, public works projects and cars. Headed by Fritz Todt, the plan initiated a number of architectural and building projects and was designed to help develop the autobahns (highways)

Hitler on his way to launch the *Wilhelm Gustloff* in May 1937 in Hamburg. This ship was the first KDF vessel and further strengthened Germany's naval muscle.

system. There was an emphasis on building up Germany's military defences – again a flagrant breach of treaty conditions.

Goering took over the Four Year Plan in October 1936 and was immediately given extraordinary powers over the situation. Basically, Goering had complete control over the German economy, including the private sector, while Hjalmar Schacht, the Minister of Economics was beginning to lose favour with the Nazi High Command due to his opposition to military expenditure. Over the following few

years, Germany began building refineries, aluminium plants and factories specifically for the development and production of synthetic materials. The Office of the Four Year Plan was considered on a par with the cabinet and even when the official four years were up in 1940 the power of the office was so great that the plan was to be continued indefinitely – the economic reforms were actually accomplished between 1941 and 1944.

An underground tunnel and guards in the Maginot Line. The French decided to extend this fortification as Germany strengthened.

In 1937, the French government were in a much better position to decide on their foreign issues. Putting aside their domestic difficulties, in February 1937, they passed a new defence plan designed to bolster the national defence system which included extending the Maginot Line along the border with Germany. The line was made of concrete and steel stretching between Luxembourg and Switzerland (along the French/German border). Built between 1930 and 1935, at a cost of 7,000 million francs, on the proposals of Joseph Joffre, the line had interdependent fortified belts with anti-tank emplacements and pillboxes in front of bombproof artillery casements.

It was named after the French War Minister, André Maginot and was said to be an impregnable defence against the Germany army following the events of the First World War. The line would matter little in the long run when Hitler's army invaded France through the heavily wooded and mountainous region of the Ardennes just north of the Maginot Line. The French had been confident that the Ardennes was impassable for German tanks – but they were to be proved wrong in 1940.

Two months after the French decided to strengthen their defences, the Germans bombed the market town of Guernica in Spain on 27 April 1937. It was to become an

The Spanish town of Guernica was completely destroyed by the German Condor Legion in an air raid in April 1937.

everlasting symbol of the atrocity of war. The reason that Germany decided to attack the sleepy market town at that time was to try out an experiment in exactly what it would take to bomb a city into oblivion. With the Spanish Civil War in full flow, it gave the Nazis an opportunity to put the German air force to the test while providing the crews with bombing experience. More than 1,650 people lost their lives in the "experiment" and the city was left entirely destroyed. The world was shocked at the enormity of the tragedy which was immortalized by Pablo Picasso's painting, *Guernica.*

Next, it was the turn of the residents of the Sudetenland in Czechoslovakia, to suffer. On 17 October 1937, pro-German riots broke out in the former German Confederation. The area had been part of Germany until

1806 and of the German Confederation between 1815 and 1866. The Sudetenland became part of Czechoslovakia following the First World War. Things had remained relatively settled until 1935 when the Sudeten-German Party, established with funds from Nazi Germany, complained that the Czech government was discriminating against the Sudeten Germans. Those who had lost their jobs during the depression argued that they would be better off under Hitler. Unrest and unease at events and treatment led to riots a year later which would further enhance the power of the Führer.

Then in November 1937, Italy made its pledge to join the Anti-Comintern Pact with Germany and Japan. Relations between Italy and Britain were strained and tense following the fascist country's invasion of Abyssinia. But, although both France and Britain were opposed to Italy's invasion, secret negotiations to give the invaders two-thirds of Abyssinia were eventually agreed in the Hoare-Laval Pact.

News of the pact was leaked to both the British and French people who were disgusted with the underhand antics of their respective governments. The Pact was subsequently withdrawn and Italy realized that neither country would be as accommodating in future – it therefore chose to ally itself with Germany.

With Goering controlling the economic affairs of Germany, the Minister for Economics, Hjalmar Schacht was fast losing control. On 24 November 1937 he lost his job at the ministry and his life took a downward turn when he was eventually released from his service to the Nazi government in 1939. In fact, he spent the remainder of the Second World War in a concentration camp before being

Hjalmar Schacht.

tried at Nuremberg for his role in the war economy. Schacht was acquitted of the accusations made against him.

But Schacht wasn't the only high-ranking official that Hitler wanted to be rid of in his quest for war. He wanted more control over the armed forces and set about removing top military commanders in order to make this possible. Prior to this, many top military personnel had welcomed Hitler's rise to power, wrongly assuming that they could manipulate their new leader for their own ends. But Hitler removed the moderate elements from the army and all the influence they had exerted and on 4 February 1938 he dismissed Blomberg and Fritsch, two top commanders in the first step to purge his forces of their leading men. Many high-ranking military personnel had been fairly diplomatic in their approach and had kept a tight reign on younger, more aggressive Nazi army troops. The German Foreign Minister, Baron von Neurath resigned his position and was replaced by Joachim von Ribbentrop who had already proved himself to Hitler by devising a new Nazi foreign policy which had led to the agreement with the British over a German naval force. By May 1938, the army leaders were made aware of Hitler's plans to invade Czechoslovakia – even though this could ultimately lead to war with Britain, France and the Soviet Union. General Ludwig Beck, the Army Chief of Staff, believed the plan to be reckless and immoral and he firmly believed that Germany would not win the war. He sent emissaries to both London and Paris in order to dissuade each government to resist Hitler's demands. The British and the French ignored all the messages from Germany as they were unsure what to make of them. At a meeting in August that same year, Beck spoke openly to a group of

Hitler is welcomed by a guard of honour at Innsbruck station following the annexation of Austria in March 1938.

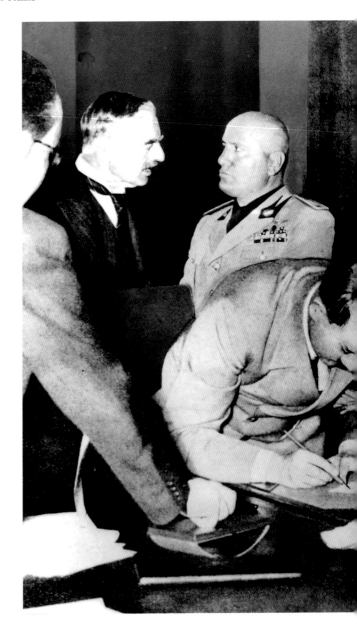

Hitler signs the Munich Agreement in September 1938, a treaty between Germany, England, Italy and France that was supposed to solve the Sudetenland crisis. Mussolini is in the background talking to British Prime Minister Neville Chamberlain.

army generals in Berlin about his opposition to war over Czechoslovakia. Hitler demanded Beck's resignation which was duly given and the German army were left in shock at their leader's sudden departure.

Just prior to this, in February 1938, Hitler had ordered the release of imprisoned Austrian Nazis. In a further attempt to take control he then abruptly invaded Austria and made it part of the German Reich by means of *Anschluss* (annexation). In April 1938, the fascist Spanish dictator, Franco, signed the Anti-Comintern Pact. Things were steadily gathering pace and on 12 August, Hitler ordered the mobilization of the German army. Exactly one month later, in September, more trouble broke out in Sudetenland in Czechoslovakia which ended with the Munich Agreement and the German annexation of large areas of western Czechoslovakia. It was designed to

Jubilant crowds greet Hitler on his return to Berlin after the signing of the Munich accord and the invasion of the Sudetenland by German troops in October 1938.

appease the western allies and for a time it worked. Signed in the early hours of 30 September 1938 in Munich, the Agreement involved all the major powers of Europe. The Czechs, however, were not invited to attend the conference and many came to regard the signed paper as the Munich Dictate. After Hitler's territorial demands were met, Czechoslovakia was divided between Germany (where

The synagogue in Prinzregentstrasse 69–70, Berlin, burns following *Kristallnacht* – a night of Nazi-organised attacks against Jewish citizens.

Sudetenland had a huge strategic importance because of its border defences), Poland and Hungary. Once again, however, it would not be long before Hitler made the decision to violate the terms of the agreement.

Still, none of the powers in western Europe wanted war and Soviet dictator Joseph Stalin and Soviet Russia were unprepared materially and politically for war. Mussolini was also unprepared for a Europe-wide conflict and was growing ever warier of Germany's increasing power. Even the German military knew that their armed forces were not up to a full-blown war and did all they could to avoid it. But propaganda was helping the cause – if at that stage superficially – and an egotistical Joseph Goebbels was desperate to take Hitler in his chosen direction. Instigated by Goebbels, *Kristallnacht* took place on 9 November 1938 following the assassination in Paris of the German embassy official Ernst von Rath.

In Britain, a delighted Prime Minister waved the agreement at an ecstatic reception on his return. It was here that Chamberlain made his "Peace for our Time" speech. The French were also pleased with the Munich Agreement, as were the German military. Hitler, meanwhile, was furious. Stalin was equally displeased. The Soviet Union had not been represented at the conference and felt that the Soviets should be recognized as a major power. It was Stalin's fear that Britain and France would sign agreements with Nazi Germany allowing partition of the USSR between western powers that convinced him to sign the Molotov–Ribbentrop Pact with Germany in 1939. When Hitler marched his army back into Czechoslovakia on 15 March 1939 and occupied the remainder of Bohemia and Moravia, Winston Churchill's prediction that the Munich

Agreement was the start of a disaster of great magnitude proved right. Chamberlain had felt betrayed by the Nazi seizure of Czechoslovakia and began to take a much harder line against Hitler. He immediately mobilized the British Empire's armed forces in preparation for war. France followed suit. Italy was fast becoming a second-rate member of the Axis and retaliated by invading Albania in April 1939.

On 1 September 1939, Germany invaded Poland. The Polish army was subsequently defeated (within weeks) and Germany began to tighten its grip. From East Prussia and Germany in the north and Silesia and Slovakia to the south, the German army with more than 2,000 tanks and more than 1,000 aircraft broke through the Polish defences and advanced on Warsaw in a massive attack from all sides. Warsaw surrendered to the Germans on 28 September 1939 after a great deal of heavy shelling and bombing. Two days after Hitler had ordered his troops into Poland, the British and French declared war on Germany.

Hitler declares his foreign policy in front of the Reichstag on 29 April 1939, including termination of the Anglo-German naval agreement and the non-aggression pact with Poland.

Chapter 7

Blitzkrieg and the Second World War

Blitzkrieg was a word which was to become synonymous with the Second World War. Meaning "lightning war", it was first used by Western newspaper journalists to describe the unbelievable speed and ferocity of the German attack on Poland on the first day of September in 1939.

The German people had given Adolf Hitler a huge show of faith by turning out in their droves for his fiftieth birthday celebrations in April 1939.

Nothing like this had been seen before, yet its foundations could be traced right back to the 1920s in the wake of Germany's military reforms after the First World War which saw Heinz Guderian emerge as a leading advocate for the use of mechanized forces such as the tank. Alongside his colleagues, Guderian took part in theoretical and practical exercises aimed at proving that the tank was the most decisive weapon of war. He did all this under a great deal of opposition from many German officers who not only gave precedence to the infantry but who were also deeply suspicious of the value of the tank. However, Guderian remained convinced that it was the tank which, if properly deployed, was without doubt, the best possible

Hitler gives a speech in the Reichstag at 10.00 am on 1 September 1939 which cited alleged Polish attacks as a justification for the invasion of Poland.

means of launching a land attack. Pointing to the experiences of the First World War, he cited the fact that an infantry-based attack made it easier for any defence barriers to be reinforced which would hamper progress. Therefore, the use of the tank would enable troops to advance far more quickly into enemy territory and to keep moving forward once each breakthrough was achieved. And, thus, the Panzer tank was born together with radio communication to help with the co-ordination and command, which Guderian said was just as fundamentally important to the success of this super-fast and powerful strategy.

It was not long before Hitler realized its potential when, after reading Guderian's book entitled *Achtung! Panzer* and witnessing some field exercises, he remarked: "That is what I want – and that is what I will have."

To sum up the principles of *Blitzkrieg* operations, its philosophy lay in its use of manoeuvre rather than stealth and attrition to outwit opponents using a combination of tank armoury, mechanized infantry, radio communication, self-propelled artillery and close air support. This strategy, which had never been seen before, was in complete contrast to the First World War.

New tactics included interrupting the enemy's communications, logistics and decision-making capabilities which reduced morale to such an extent that the slower, defending forces had little option but to retreat into concentrated defensive zones which were then encircled and reduced by the German infantry following up behind. Once the attack point had been identified and the main armoured force had penetrated, striking at lightning speed, the motorized infantry would fan out behind to capture and destroy the enemy forces which were trapped within the encircling massed ranks of Panzer tanks with

German infantry advance into Poland, September 1939.

overhead air power ensuring that no escape was possible giving the enemy no option but to surrender.

Hitler had, by now, developed a thirst for obtaining more land, especially to the east of Germany, initially, and he used the severe restrictions that had been placed upon Germany by the Treaty of Versailles as a pretext for Germany's "right" to acquire more land where German-speaking people lived. On 13 March 1938, Germany annexed Austria, which was forbidden by the Treaty of Versailles. Just six months later, Britain and France, not fully realizing that Hitler had much greater ambitions in amassing vast swathes of land, handed him a large section of Czechoslovakia but, by March 1939, he had taken over the rest of the country. In hindsight, this begs the question of why Britain and France had allowed Hitler to take over these two countries without a fight?

It was their assumption, which turned out to be wrong, that a few concessions to Hitler would be a worthwhile price to pay to avoid the bloodshed that was witnessed in the First World War. Little did Britain and France realize at

The *Schleswig-Holstein* shells Danzig into submission.

that time that Hitler had far more grandiose schemes planned. His acquisition of land had only just begun and, with the Nazi-Soviet Non-Aggression Pact, Hitler had set his sights on acquiring Poland, calculating that he could do this without having to fight Britain and France. However, he still needed an excuse so that he would not be perceived as the aggressor. Fortunately for Hitler, his comrade Heinrich Himmler had come up with the perfect plan.

On 31 August 1939, the Nazis took an unknown prisoner from one of their concentration camps and they forced him to put on a Polish uniform. He was then driven to the town of Gleiwitz, which was situated on the border between Poland and Germany, where he was shot dead. The Germans had staged this to appear as a Polish attack

German soldiers remove the Polish border markings in Upper Silesia in September 1939.

against a German radio station. Just a few hours later, at precisely 4.45 am on 1 September 1939, German troops entered Poland for the first time. Its air attack was so sudden and fierce that most of the Polish Air Force's planes were destroyed before they could even get airborne.

There was little hope of Poland mobilizing its troops quickly as both bridges and roads were taken out by bombing raids and the Polish infantry were simply machine-gunned from the air. But the Germans didn't just target the Polish military. Ordinary civilians trying to flee their homes were also mercilessly gunned down. *Blitzkrieg* was being witnessed for the very first time with the Germans causing as much chaos and confusion as they could to prevent Poland from mobilizing its forces quickly.

On the ground, the Germans had sixty-two divisions invading Poland by land, six of which were armoured, and ten that were mechanized. And, although Poland had forty divisions of its own, the surprise and speed of the attack and the fact that almost their entire force had been completely destroyed alongside their cavalry, which was simply no match for the German tanks meant that, with no armoured divisions, they had no chance of competing against the hitherto unimaginable magnitude and ferocity of the German attack.

Later that same day, Britain and France, having woken up to the reality of what had taken place, issued Hitler with an ultimatum: either to withdraw his forces from Poland or face war with both Britain and France. Two days later on 3 September, and with Germany's forces penetrating ever deeper into Polish territory, both Britain and France declared war on Germany. However, over in Poland, the Germans were now using more conventional

and traditional methods on the ground with artillery and infantry forces focused on crushing any resistance.

In April and May of 1940, Hitler was ready to flex his military might even further afield, beginning in Norway and Denmark where the Germans invaded and took control in order to safeguard supply routes of Swedish ore while establishing a Norwegian base aimed at breaking the British naval blockade on Germany. Once that was achieved, Hitler's focus, more ominously, came back towards Western Europe where the *blitzkrieg* tactics were deployed again to devastating effect in Luxembourg, Belgium and Holland. All of these countries came under Nazi occupation, with Rotterdam in Holland, being bombed almost to rubble. It was at this time, too, that

The German victory parade in Warsaw on 5 October 1939.

The *Wehrmacht* march into Denmark in 1940. An anti-aircraft soldier protects the advancing troops and vehicles.

France was to come up against Hitler's military might in the form of a lightning-fast invasion which was to end with the desperate evacuation from Dunkirk.

The combined invasion of France, Belgium and Holland was made up of two phases – Operation Yellow (*Fall Gelb*) and Operation Red (*Fall Rot*). Yellow opened up with a sortie conducted by paratroopers and two armoured corps against both Holland and Belgium. The main bulk of the German armoured force was massed within their primary tank division, Panzer Group von Kleist, which broke through at a relatively unguarded sector in the Ardennes and, with help from the air force took Sedan.

From there, the group then started their march towards the coast of the English Channel at Abbéville. In doing this, it isolated the Belgian Army, the British Expeditionary Force and some divisions within the French army who

France fell to the Germans in 1940. This photograph shows a pair of Messerschmitt ME 110s flying past the Eiffel Tower in Paris.

were based up in northern France. In fact, such was the progress of the Nazi forces at this juncture, which had far surpassed their own expectations, that the German commanders began to get a little nervous and concerned about having gone too far, too quickly. This fear soon became a reality when the group were met at Arras with a counter-attack by a British motorized force armed with heavy Matilda tanks which forced the Nazis to halt, on instructions from Hitler, just outside the port city of Dunkirk, which the Allies were using to evacuate its troops. And, although the head of the Luftwaffe, Hermann Goering, gave Hitler his assurance that his air force would completely obliterate the Allied forces who were about to evacuate, that never worked out quite in accordance with Goering's plans and, in Operation Dynamo, thanks to the Allied defence and resistance, over 330,000 French, British, Dutch, Belgian and Polish troops were saved.

British and French troops on the beach at Dunkirk waiting for ships to take them to safety after the advance of the Wehrmacht.

The Yellow team exceeded everybody's expectations despite claims that the Germans had almost 2,000 armoured vehicles fewer than the combined armoured forces of the Allies. Even with those odds stacked against the Germans, they still left the French armies without much of their own armour and heavy equipment.

Operation Red then launched a three-pronged attack with
XV Panzer Corps advancing on Brest, XIV Panzer Corps
involved in attacking areas east of Paris, and Guderian's
XIX Panzer Corps completing the surrounding of the
Maginot Line and all this was achieved with little
resistance from the defending forces. Guderian's original

predictions all those years previously were borne out starkly during this period with the French nation and army capitulating within two months of the *blitzkrieg* attack having been launched as opposed to the four years of trench warfare of the First World War.

Following Dunkirk, it would be barely two months before Hitler embarked on his most audacious and ambitious scheme yet which brought Britain right into the firing line. Dubbed the "Battle of Britain", it would become one of the most heroic episodes of resistance to Nazi might of the entire war.

Now that France had fallen, only the English Channel and the North Sea separated Britain from further advance of the Nazi forces. Anticipating that the war would now have to be fought in the air first if the Germans were to stand any hope of capturing and occupying Britain on the ground, the RAF were faced with a rapid programme of building as many new planes as it could in order to try to repel the mighty Luftwaffe. Hitler and his military

British troops embark on their rescue transport at Dunkirk. The operation to evacuate as many troops as possible saw the largest flotilla of naval and private vessels in history sail to France.

commanders held the mistaken belief that such was the Luftwaffe's superiority in the air that the plans they drew up for "Operation Sealion" were to completely wipe out the RAF within just four weeks. During this period, the initial focus was to destroy all of the RAF's bases and infrastructure while their fighter planes were to engage the RAF to destroy their planes in the air.

The preliminary action began over late July and into early August in 1940 with a series of raids over the English Channel. But it was on 13 August, that the attacks increased in intensity when the Luftwaffe launched their first major assault on the RAF. Their initial targets were radar stations and airfields close to the southern English

The destruction around St Paul's Cathedral in London caused by German aerial attacks is clearly evident.

British pilots
scramble in the
face of an
incoming German
raid.

coast and while the Luftwaffe made steady ground moving further inland, their raids at this stage proved relatively ineffective as the radar stations were quickly repaired. It was ten days later on 23 August that it decided

The bombing of
London's Victoria
Docks in
September 1940.

to switch its approach and take on the responsibility of trying to destroy the RAF's Fighter Command. This was a pivotal moment in the Battle of Britain which ultimately turned out to be the turning point as to whether or not Britain survived. Initially, the Luftwaffe were in the ascendancy hammering at the principle Fighter Command airfields as the RAF desperately tried to defend itself against wave after wave of attacks. But with its Hawker Hurricanes and Supermarine Spitfires, combined with the ability to use radar to give advance warning of the enemy, the RAF fought back.

Having grossly underestimated the extent of Britain's intelligence from its sophisticated radar detection system, the Luftwaffe's tactics became more haphazard and this, alongside the Spitfire's ability to outmanoeuvre the Luftwaffe's twin-engined BF 110, meant that it had to deploy escorts for its planes and it was soon becoming apparent that the RAF were inflicting a heavy toll of

German fighters approach the English coast.

A squadron of
Heinkel He-111
bombers on a
mission over
England in 1940.

casualties on the Luftwaffe and that British resistance under fierce attack was proving far more stubborn than even Hitler and Himmler could have possibly envisaged.

With German morale beginning to dip, Hitler realized that he needed to adopt a different tactic if there was to be any hope of winning this battle, so the next phase began when he ordered the Luftwaffe to turn its attention to bombing major British cities, in the hope of destroying civilian morale. The Luftwaffe's offensive included numerous raids on British cities in July and August which killed more than 1,250 civilians, yet Hitler had issued a strict directive that London was not to be targeted at this stage except upon his sole instructions. It wasn't long, however, before this directive was issued and the capital and other major British cities became legitimate targets with Hitler's blessing.

This was a direct response to Britain's bombing of Berlin, yet Hitler was not aware that the bombing of the Fighter Command bases had forced the RAF to consider withdrawing from south-eastern England.

On 7 September 1940, a wave of attacks which involved almost 400 bombers and over 600 fighter planes targeted the docks in London's East End. However, with the focus having switched from the Fighter Command bases to the cities, this tactic employed by Hitler had inadvertently given time for a battered and weary RAF to regroup and return in even greater numbers which took the Luftwaffe by surprise. Nevertheless, their campaign of bombing Britain continued with attacks on cities as far afield as Manchester, Glasgow, Liverpool, Coventry and Plymouth – the latter two suffering the most.

The raids were even more frightening because, following the failure of daytime raids in making any real impact, they switched tactics and began bombing at night to lessen the likelihood of planes being shot down. However, the Luftwaffe's losses were beginning to take their toll. As it switched its attention to attacking more northerly cities in Britain, it began to realize the limitations of its aircraft which, in making these longer sorties, had barely ten minutes in which to carry out raids before their fuel capacity forced them to turn for home. Morale was

Hermann Goering and his fellow officers watch the Operation Sealion attacks of October 1940 against England from the coast of France.

The view from
inside a Heinkel
He-111 as a
Spitfire attacks in
March 1941.

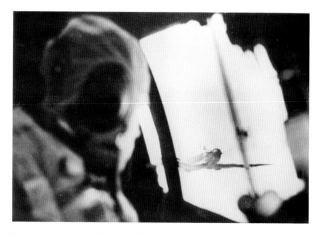

further weakened when the Germans discovered that RAF
Bomber Command had added to German problems by
sinking eighty invasion barges in the port of Ostend.

It was becoming obvious to Hitler that the RAF was
putting up more of a fight than he had envisaged and, on
11 September, he announced a postponement of Operation
Sealion until thirteen days later on 24 September. It was
short-lived, and on 15 September, the Luftwaffe took to the
skies again in two massive waves of attacks, but the RAF
was ready and waiting and made use of every single
aircraft in its 11 Group Squadron that day. The outcome
was to prove a critical juncture in the Battle of Britain.
While eighty-six planes were shot down that day, sixty of
them were German.

There was no getting away from the fact that the RAF
was now more than capable of defending British skies.
And, with the Luftwaffe reeling from the loss of so many
men and aircraft while lacking adequate replacements,
Hitler was left with little alternative but to announce a
postponement of any invasion until the spring of 1941.

By the end of October, all air raids had ceased and the RAF could say that it had triumphed against all the odds in the Battle of Britain. The renewed assault in spring never materialized and the threat finally ended with Hitler's Directive 21 on 18 December 1940 which focused German efforts away from Britain towards the Soviet Union in what would become Operation Barbarossa six months down the line.

Prior to that assault, however, there were still issues to resolve elsewhere. With the help of Italian troops who had declared war on Britain and France in June 1940, the Germans attacked and defeated the armies of Yugoslavia and Greece which, while they fought bravely, lacked the military capacity to combat Germany's power and mobility. At first glance, it might appear odd that Italy became an ally of Germany. It is true that at first, they were very much opposed to the idea of Germany's expansion

German tanks advance on the Soviet border in Operation Barbarossa in mid 1941.

Red Army troops
are surprised by
the German attack
on the Soviet
Union and
surrender.

and, in fact, they positioned troops close to the Austrian
border and had been prepared to declare war on Germany
as they were opposed to the German occupation.

However, during a conference between Britain, France and Italy, who had been old allies during the First World War, the three countries fell out over Britain's decision to sign the Anglo-German Naval Pact, and Italy took its revenge by giving its consent to German expansion into Austria. The two countries became even closer after Italy was punished by the League of Nations for invading Abyssinia in 1936. It had its trading rights revoked which Germany alone ignored leading to a strengthening friendship which was later formalized by the signing of the Rome–Berlin Axis which almost secured an alliance. However, when the British drove the Italians out of Egypt, Hitler came to their support in Libya.

The *Bismarck* was sunk by British ships in May 1941 in the North Atlantic.

The operations in Africa were led by one of Germany's most famous commanders, Erwin Rommel. Nicknamed "The Desert Fox", he became engaged in a battle for supremacy in the region between 1941 and 1943 and the subsequent battles over this period, with his British counterpart Field Marshal Montgomery, have since become legendary. The famous Battle of El Alamein which began in October 1942 and lasted for twelve days was the first Allied land victory of the war. Had Hitler's attention not been fully taken up by the Soviet Union at the time, he may have provided Rommel with an adequate number of troops a year or so earlier, in which case the Desert Fox may well have driven the British forces out of Egypt.

The Russian weather played havoc with Germany's plan's to conquer the Soviet Union. Here a convoy is stuck in the mud in the spring of 1942.

General Erwin Rommel was one of the great tacticians in the German army but even he was unable to ultimately secure victory in Africa.

Back in Europe, Operation Barbarossa was to take the Soviet Union completely by surprise, especially as the Soviet Union had signed a treaty with Germany back in 1939. Hitler sent three million soldiers and over 350,000 tanks into the Soviet Union and although the Russians had an even greater number of tanks, most of them were obsolete and Germany was able to gain a great amount of territory taking them nearly to Moscow.

This period of the war saw an incredible 20 million casualties and Stalin's regime seemed to be powerless to stop the might of the German forces as they advanced on Moscow. Stalin's brutal Communist regime had already committed political mass murder in getting rid of nearly all its most senior officers before the war and its lack of modern equipment coupled with a rigid Communist attitude towards its remaining officers looked like proving to be the Soviet Union's downfall. It was only at the eleventh hour, when Georgy Zhukov, who had fallen out with Stalin previously, but who had a great command of logistics, was put in command and was able to persuade

Stalin to introduce a new breed of battle-hardened younger commanders, equipped with new weapons that the Red Army became stronger.

This enabled the Red Army to force the Nazis back from Moscow. In the end, the Nazis simply couldn't match Russian supplies, nor could they cope with the vast size of the Soviet Union and its extreme weather conditions. Not only were they were forced to retreat, but Soviet forces went on the offensive and started to recapture the land which had previously been lost. They did not stop there, but continued to advance ultimately all the way to Berlin where they brought about Hitler's final downfall and the end of the Second World War.

With the Nazis in retreat, and Soviet forces advancing as a result of the failure of Operation Barbarossa, the Allies were given a further boost when they were joined by the United States, following the Japanese attack on Pearl Harbor on 7 December 1941, which forced both Britain and

The unprovoked attack on Pearl Harbor by the Japanese brought the United States into the war and Germany found its opponents strengthened by the massive additional resources.

the United States to declare war on Japan. In spite of the Japanese capturing Singapore from Britain, it's ultimate downfall came with the Battle of Midway in June 1942.

Meanwhile, over in Africa, in November 1942, the combined forces of both the British and American troops, led by US General Dwight Eisenhower, had assumed control of Algeria and French Morocco. They were gradually moving in on the Germans and less than six months later, in May 1943, the Germans were forced to surrender in Africa.

The momentum was now very much with the Allies. Defeat in Africa by the Allies combined with the Red Army defeating the Nazis at Stalingrad was to be followed with the British and American forces taking Sicily and the subsequent surrender of Italy in September 1943. By January 1944, the Red Army had regained control of Leningrad, and Rome was finally liberated from the Germans in June, in spite of the fact that Italy had surrendered some nine months earlier.

The campaign to liberate Western Europe continued with the D-Day landings of June 1944, which marked the beginning of the end of the Nazi occupation.

A paratrooper directs a convoy in Rome after the German offensive following the armistice between Italy and the Allies on 3 September 1943.

Chapter 8

Occupied Europe and Nazi atrocities

From the outset of the Second World War when the Germans invaded Poland on 1 September 1939, it was clear that accepted rules of engagement on the battlefield formed no part of the Nazis thinking. Before the end of October in Poland, they had systematically dropped bombs on hospitals, executed Polish prisoners of war, shot refugees, murdered civilians and even killed soldiers who were wounded and who presented no further threat to them. In less than two months, it was estimated that at least 16,000 people, both soldiers and civilians, had been butchered.

Polish civilians and soldiers killed by German troops in Ciepielov, September 1939.

This was an ominous warning which culminated in the Holocaust, a genocide unparalleled in history. The Holocaust was symptomatic of the many other atrocities which took place across Europe as the Nazis instituted their brutal occupation.

Jews in an assembly camp in Poland in the autumn of 1939.

While the true extent of all of the atrocities that took place between 1939 and the end of the war in 1945 could never be condensed into one single chapter, the following accounts will starkly illustrate just some of the carnage that the Nazis inflicted on the people of several European

It was not only the Nazis who were guilty of atrocities. Here, Germans discover a mass grave in Katyn, Poland, in April 1943. It is estimated that around 15,000 Polish officers were murdered by Stalin's secret police in September 1939.

countries over the course of six years. What will be described is just the tip of the iceberg and is, by no means, a comprehensive account of all of the atrocities that took place, nor are they necessarily the most horrific. They all serve to demonstrate, though, how the Nazis would stop at nothing in the pursuit of their genocidal aims.

Poland

Once the Nazis had taken over Poland, they embarked on a series of raids on its towns and villages. In a process which they termed "pacification", they would randomly round up a few hundred people from each town or village and march them to a designated place where pits had been dug. There, the victims were forced to undress and lie face down before being shot dead. Their bodies were then covered in a layer of quicklime before a second group was ordered to lie on top of the dead bodies to be executed in the same way.

This horrific procedure would continue until the pit was full. Layer upon layer of butchered corpses would then be trampled down by the Nazis until the top layer was level and then trees and grass would be planted on top of the pile. Such executions would be repeated in other parts of Poland and, later on, in the Soviet Union. In another incident in the Polish village of Szalas, over 300 males, some as young as fifteen, were machine-gunned to death and others were simply locked up in a local school which was then set ablaze.

In the region known as Pomerania, in the town of Bydogszcz (Bromberg), it is estimated that over 10,000 non-Jewish Polish civilians were murdered within the first four months of the Nazi occupation. Lawyers, priests, teachers and industrial leaders were rounded up and

Polish civilians being executed by German troops in the immediate aftermath of the occupation.

machine-gunned to death in the town square and around 100 boy scouts, aged between twelve and sixteen, suffered a similar fate on the steps of a Jesuit church. Hitler had become a proponent of tit for tat killings at this point, and announced that for every German killed, a figure of between fifty and 100 Poles would be executed in retaliation. No-one was spared. Over 3,700 patients in a mental hospital were shot dead and in Pomerania, out of 650 members of the clergy, only 20 priests were spared with the rest either being shot or taken to concentration camps.

The Warsaw Uprising, which began on 1 August 1944, was the Polish Home Army's attempt to liberate Warsaw from German occupation. Initially, it was only meant to last for a few days until Soviet troops could reach the city,

Warsaw was left in ruins following the Uprising in late 1944.

but they stopped short. The Poles wanted to secure their freedom before Soviet troops arrived to try to establish control over the city. However, by the time the Polish Army was forced to surrender over two months later on 2 October, there had been a staggering number of civilian deaths as a result of mass murders carried out by the retreating German troops. The scale of the killing was so great that it has been virtually impossible to establish how many died; estimates range from 120,000 to 250,000. In just one day, 11 September 1944, more than 50,000 civilians were executed.

Once the Polish Army had surrendered, the German troops burned down the city, block by block. Together, with earlier damage inflicted at the beginning of the war in 1939, it is thought that over eighty-five per cent of the city of Warsaw was destroyed in the course of the war.

Czechoslovakia

On 27 May, 1942, Jan Kubis and Joseph Gabeik, two Czech patriots serving with the Polish forces in Britain, volunteered to undertake a daring mission to assassinate Reinhard Heydrich, the SS *Obergruppen-führer* who was the Reich Protector of Bohemia and Moravia. They were dropped by parachute near Prague, and the ambush took place as Heydrich was driving to his office. He was severely wounded and rushed to hospital but died eight days later. The Nazi reprisals were not long in coming.

Over the next few days, over 3,000 Czech citizens were arrested, of whom over 1,300 were shot dead. A further 657 died at the hands of the SS while being interrogated. Then, on 9 June, armed police surrounded the tiny village of Lidice, about 10km from Prague, and rounded up the

The Germans destroyed the village of Lidice as a reprisal for the assassination of Reinhard Heydrich in 1942.

entire population, herding them all into the small village square. All the men and any boys over the age of fifteen were taken to an empty barn and locked in while all females and the remaining younger males were kept in the local school. The Nazis then ransacked all the houses, gathering up all the mattresses. The following morning, all the women and younger children were loaded onto trucks and driven away to camps. The mattresses were then propped up against the barn walls and ten males at a time would be brought to stand against them to be shot dead. The final death toll was 173 and, while this brutal slaying was in progress, the rest of the Nazi troops set the entire village on fire and razed it to the ground using ploughs and bulldozers until it was completely unrecognizable.

Two weeks later, the small Czech village of Lezaky was also destroyed, with the Nazis randomly shooting dead both men and women. The remaining children were either taken to concentration camps or "Aryanised". Altogether, it is estimated that around 1,300 lost their lives as a result of the Nazis Party's determination to gain revenge for the death of Heydrich.

Belgium

Towards the end of the war on 5 September 1944, following the Nazis' recapture of the village of Bande, during the Ardennes Offensive, a unit of the German SD (*Sicherheitsdienst*), arrested all the men in the village. The purpose was to question them about events which had taken place there three months earlier, when a unit of Belgian soldiers had attacked a German unit, killing three Nazi soldiers in the process.

One by one, they were lined up in front of a local café, questioned and then led to the open door. As they were forced to walk inside, one by one, they were killed with a shot to the neck at point blank range by an SD soldier who was positioned just inside the doorway. As they fell dead to the ground, it was also the soldier's job to send them down into the cellar with a kick.

One of the most notorious of the atrocities perpetrated by the Nazis during the Second World War was against US prisoners of war during the Battle of the Bulge. The Malmédy Massacre, which took place on 17 December 1944, was the work of the 1ˢᵗ SS Panzer Division led by *Kampfgruppe* Peiper. On its way to join up with the US 7ᵗʰ Armored Division in Sankt Vith, to which it was attached, a US convoy from the 285ᵗʰ Field Artillery Observation Battalion (FAOB) was intercepted by Peiper's group which opened fire and forced it to stop. The Americans, with only rifles and small arms with which to defend themselves, were forced to surrender. One hundred and twenty US troops were marched into a nearby field where they were executed.

While the Germans later tried to explain the mass slaughter as the result of some American prisoners trying to escape and others having miraculously recovered their weapons, the truth began to emerge when eighty-eight of the bodies were recovered a month later. On examination, the vast majority were found to have single gunshot wounds to the head, more consistent with a mass execution than with an attempt to prevent them escaping or an act of self-defence.

Other autopsies performed that day concluded that those who had not died through a single gunshot to the head at close range had suffered fatal blows to the head consistent with a rifle butt being smashed against the head. A few who had managed to escape sought refuge in a

A war crimes trial before a US military tribunal in Dachau. Samuel Bobyns searches amongst those accused for the person who saved him from being shot near Malmédy.

nearby café but that was set alight by the Nazis and any US soldiers who tried to make a run from the flames were simply gunned down.

France

On 27 and 28 May 1940 at Pas-de-Calais, around 100 British troops of the Cheshire Regiment, the 2nd Royal Warwickshire Regiment and the Royal Artillery were taken prisoner by No 7 Company, 2nd Battalion of the SS *Leibstandarte* Adolf Hitler. At Esquelberg, close to the town of Wormhoudt, which was situated about twelve miles from Dunkirk, the British troops were forced to march across fields to a nearby farm where they were all forced

The bodies of French civilians killed by the advancing German troops in 1940 are evidence of the brutality with which the invasion was carried out.

217

German snipers
fire on French
civilians in the
Place de la
Concorde during
the liberation of
Paris in August
1944.

into a barn so small that not even the wounded were able to lie down. Then, stick grenades were thrown into the barn which resulted in carnage. The prisoners suffered an agonising death from shrapnel wounds. The few who were left standing at the end of this massacre were forced outside, in batches of five, where they were executed.

Although the D-Day landings in Normandy would ultimately prove to be the beginning of the end for the Nazis, their surrender would not come easily and it would take almost another year to drive them all the way back to Berlin, and their final defeat.

Within the many battles that ensued in Normandy that summer, on 8 June the Allies learned that thirty-seven Canadian soldiers had been captured by the 2nd Battalion of the 26th Panzer Grenadier Regiment and taken to its army headquarters. From there, they were taken to the village of Le Mesnil-Patty where they were forced to sit down in a field with their wounded in the centre. Shortly afterwards, a group of SS soldiers arrived and, armed with machine pistols, walked towards the group and systematically shot them dead. Two of the soldiers managed to escape, although they were later recaptured and spent the remainder of the war in a POW camp. In the nearby villages of Buron and Authie, another forty Canadian soldiers were rounded up and one by one, as they were being marched back to the rear, a number of them were told to remove their helmets and were then shot dead with automatic rifles. Their bodies were then dragged out into the middle of the road where they were left to be run over by German tanks and trucks. Some French civilians went and recovered what remained of the bodies, dragging them back towards the pavement but were ordered to put them back onto the road again.

Over 7 and 8 June 1944, twenty of the remaining Canadian prisoners were locked up in a stable in the grounds of the Abbaye Ardenne. One by one, they were called by name and, as they emerged from the doorway, they were shot in the back of the head. On 8 June, a further twenty-six Canadians were shot dead at the Chateau d'Audrie by another unit of German forces called the SS *Hitler Jugend* who became known as the "Murder Division".

Two days later on 10 June, while heading north towards the Normandy invasion, a unit of the 2nd Panzer Division *Das Reich* under the command of SS General Lammerding, arrived at Oradour-sur-Glane. Here, the 120-man SS unit surrounded the village and ordered all of its residents to go to the market place where they were to undergo an identity check. Ominously, as has already been

described in some of the earlier accounts here, the men
were separated from the women and children. While the
latter were rounded up and taken to a nearby church, the
men were divided into six groups and taken to six separate
barns and local garages where they were shot. Not content
with this, the Germans proceeded to cover their dead
corpses with straw, which was then set ablaze. This time,
however, the women and children were not to be spared.
Just over 450 of them huddled in the church died when
smoke grenades were hurled through the windows, along
with shrapnel grenades all accompanied by machine gun
fire throughout. They never stood a chance and when the
massacre was over, the church was then set on fire.

The village of Oradour-sur-Glane in the twenty-first century. It has never been rebuilt and today stands as a memorial to those who were massacred in 1944 as revenge for the activities of the French Resistance.

Italy

In retaliation for Italian troops defecting to the Allies, Italy, would go on to suffer many atrocities at the hands of the Nazis.

On Via Rasella in Rome on 23 March 1944, on the same day that Mussolini formed his Fascist Party, twenty-six SS men were killed and more than sixty wounded, when a bomb exploded (a further two died later). Upon hearing about the bombing, Hitler ordered that thirty Italian soldiers were to be shot for every SS policeman killed. He later reduced this figure to ten. Within the next twenty-four hours, over 330 people were loaded onto trucks and driven to nearby caves on the Via Ardeatina, which the

221

Nazis had discovered some time earlier. They were taken off the trucks, forced to kneel down and systematically shot in the back of the head. It took less than five hours to kill all the victims.

On 12 August 1944, in the village of Sant' Anna di Stazzema in Tuscany, SS soldiers of the II Battalion of SS Panzergrenadier-Regiment 35 of 16 SS-Panzergrenadier-Division Reichsführer commanded by SS-*Hauptsturmführer* Anton Galler rounded up 560 men, women and children who were then shot dead and their bodies burned. It was only as recently as June 2005, that an Italian military court in La Spezia found ten former SS officers, who were still living in Germany, guilty of involvement in this massacre whereupon they were sentenced to life imprisonment.

Greece

Greece and its islands did not to escape Nazi atrocities which were inflicted in the latter part of 1943 and in 1944. The Italian Acqui Division, led by General Antonio Gandin, which consisted of over 500 officers and more than 11,000 enlisted men, was stationed on the island of Kefalonia. On 8 September 1943, the Italian government, under the command of Marshal Pietro Badoglio, ordered Italian troops to cease hostilities against the Allies. There was much delight and celebration among the Italian troops, yet their German counterparts were not at all pleased about these developments which soon led to the Italian troops being branded "traitors" by the Nazis. This was followed by the arrival of the German 11th Battalion of the Jäger-Regiment 98 of the 1st *Gebirgs* (Mountain) Division under the leadership of Major Harald von

German forces invade Crete in May 1941.

An SS soldier shoots a civilian at the edge of a mass grave near the Ukrainian village of Vinnitsa in 1942.

Hirschfeld and it wasn't long before they began launching a series of bombing raids on the Italian positions. The fighting was quick to escalate and it soon became an all-out massacre whereby, in little more than four hours, 4,750 Italian soldiers were killed all over the island. A similar number were herded onto boats and shipped to the mainland before being transported on to Germany to serve in the labour camps. An additional 3,000 men died in the Ionian Sea where their boats sank after hitting mines.

When the Nazis finally took control of the Aegean island of Kos, they took almost 5,000 British and Italian soldiers prisoner (the Italians had, by this time, switched their allegiance to the Allies). Hitler had already decreed that any Italian officers who were captured were to be killed and so it was that on 4 October 1943, the Italian officer in charge, Colonel Felice Leggio, along with 101 of his officers were taken to a salt pan just east of the town of Kos and shot in groups of ten. It wasn't until the island of Kos was handed back to Greece after the war that the bodies, which had been buried in mass graves, could be dug up and taken back to Italy for a proper burial at the military cemetery in Bari.

The town of Kalavryta in the south of the Greek mainland was obliterated in typical Nazi fashion around two weeks before Christmas in 1943. On 13 December, a unit of the German army *Kampfgruppe Ebersberger* the 117th Jager Division, under the command of General Karl de Suire, surrounded the town and all of its inhabitants were herded into its local school. Just as in previous atrocities, the men and male youths were separated from the women and young children and made to march towards a nearby hollow on a hill. Nazi soldiers, armed with machine guns, were already lying in wait for the procession, and as they looked down upon the town which had just been set on fire, this was the signal for them to begin another round of bloody carnage upon the men and youths who were like sitting ducks as they huddled together in the hollow. Just over half an hour later, the Nazis marched back down the hill having wiped out almost 700 men and youths – the entire male population of Kalavryta. Down in the town in the late afternoon, the women and young children were finally released. It is hard to imagine how they must have felt as, in surveying the scene, now bereft of men and male youths, all that remained of a recognizable landscape was eight homes left standing out of an original 500. A memorial stands in Kalavryta today carved with the names of the 1,300 men who lost their lives that day both in the town itself and in twenty-four surrounding villages nearby.

On 10 June 1944, in little more than two hours, in the Greek village of Distomo, German troops from the 4th SS *Polizei Panzergrenadier* Division went from house to house and murdered almost 220 Greek civilians. It was not only men and male youths they targeted this time. According to accounts given by survivors later, SS forces stabbed pregnant women to death with bayonets, as well as babies sleeping in their cribs. They also beheaded the village priest.

Members of the SS and the military police of the Wehrmacht hang three Russian partisans.

These were just a few of the atrocities that took place during the Nazi occupation of Greece. In total, in this one region alone, it is estimated that around 60,000 men, women and children lost their lives and over 460 villages were destroyed.

Soviet prisoners of war are guarded in an open field. Millions perished as a result of malnutrition and exposure.

A Jewish man mourns next to the bodies of two women in Budapest in October 1944.

The true extent of the damage done by the Nazis' reign of terror will probably never be fully known. Other atrocities which were committed included the brutality with which Soviet Red Army prisoners of war were treated with over three million Soviet POWs dying in quite barbaric, unimaginable conditions, predominantly through starvation, disease and the conditions they were forced to work under in the camps.

During the Nazi campaign of extermination of the Slavic population in the occupied territories, several thousand villages were razed to the ground with entire populations being taken out. In Belarus, for example, it is estimated that only one in four of the population survived the German occupation.

Seven rows of mass graves containing around 700 bodies were unearthed in the Schwerin district of northern Germany in March 1961.

Altogether, the war claimed an estimated 50 to 70 million lives with more civilian deaths than military. Atrocities against civilians included death from shootings, explosions, suffocation, fire and starvation. The Nazis were very much the main perpetrators of this barbarism. More than six million Jews lost their lives, as did three million Soviet Union POWs. Genocide was extended to include the disabled, gypsies, homosexuals and others.

The main Nazi executioners were, without doubt, the SS, led by Heinrich Himmler. Many atrocities perpetrated by the Nazis all over Europe and beyond have been well documented. Others will remain clouded in mystery, with the truth only ever being known by those who died and the Nazi perpetrators themselves.

Russian partisans are forced by their executioners to dig their own graves.

While this book is concerned primarily with the Nazis, they were not the only ones to carry out heinous crimes. While they may have been the main protagonists of the war, conducting their activities on such a massive scale and with brutal disregard for human life, the Soviet Red Army, the Italian Fascists and the Japanese were also to prove that mankind had degenerated to a standard of behaviour which had not been witnessed before and which, hopefully, will never be witnessed again. Even the United States, by dropping two atomic bombs on Japan in August 1945 demonstrated how the war machine had changed so dramatically from the battlefields of the First World War, in proving that it had now become possible to wipe out enormous numbers of people in a split second.

Inhabitants of Kerch in the Soviet Union search for relatives amongst the bodies of those slaughtered by German troops in February 1942.

The Second World War devastated Europe. Railroads, bridges, water and sanitation systems, electric lines, and other infrastructure were in ruins. Millions of homes were reduced to rubble. Manufacturing plants, businesses and

farms were unusable. Millions of people who would have been working in these types of facilities were dead.

Sixty million refugees were made homeless by the war. An estimated eleven million civilians were butchered by the Nazis because of their race, religion, sexual preference, physical or mental disability, ideological opposition, or resistance to Nazi genocide.

After the surrender of the Nazis, Germany was divided into four zones of occupation, controlled by the United States, Britain, France, and the Soviet Union. The Allies liberated the camps but, in one last act of defiance, the Germans tried to murder as many prisoners as they could before the arrival of the Allied troops. Those who remained alive were barely recognizable with some weighing not much more than seventy pounds and thousands died, in spite of the arrival of much needed medical aid and food.

And, while six million displaced refugees were able to return to their native countries within just a few months, a further two million had to be temporarily housed in displaced person's camps.

Only a few weeks after the German surrender, an International Military Tribunal was set up in the German city of Nuremberg to try captured Nazi war criminals and other high-ranking Nazis who had eluded capture. The tribunal comprised eight judges, two each from the United States, the UK, France, and the Soviet Union. Twenty-one of twenty-four indicted Nazi leaders stood trial in the first of what would become known as the Nuremberg Trials. The charges brought against these men were conspiracy, crimes against peace, war crimes, and crimes against humanity.

Chapter 9

The Holocaust

At the end of the 1920s German Jews were fully integrated into German society; many were prosperous, active in the fields of finance, culture and science and a number had joined the German army. By 1938, however, just five years after the rise to power of Hitler and the Nazi Party, they had been virtually totally excluded from German social and political life. In the face of the relentless persecution, many German Jews sought asylum abroad.

Through anti-Semitic newspapers, radio broadcasts, and other means of propaganda aimed at alienating the Jews, their lives were utterly transformed. In 1938, more than 17,000 Polish Jews living in Germany were arrested and deported to Poland, but Polish border guards sent the deportees back across the river which marked the boundary between the two countries. The stalemate continued for days, during which time the Jews were without food and shelter in the pouring rain. Eventually the Polish authorities set up a refugee camp for the Jewish deportees, but conditions were terrible and many tried to escape. Those who succeeded and made it back to Germany were shot. But this horrific episode was merely a prelude to what was to come.

When the Third Secretary to the German Embassy in Paris, Ernst von Rath, was killed by a young Jew on 9 November 1938, the Nazis used his death as an excuse to

A young woman is ridiculed by members of the SA for her relationship with a Jew in 1935.

launch a pogrom against Jews living in Germany. *Kristallnacht*, the destruction of Jewish homes, businesses and synagogues instigated by Joseph Goebbels, took place on the night that von Rath died. Gauleiters, the SA and the SS were all involved in smashing and ransacking homes and businesses and their orders were specific: they were told not to harm any non-Jewish people, and not to destroy any property belonging to them. Armed with sledgehammers and axes, the perpetrators were intent on attacking Jews only. They also had orders to arrest young, healthy Jewish males. Around 200 Jews were killed or committed suicide on *Kristallnacht*, named for all the broken glass left in the streets in the aftermath of the attacks. Similar pogroms received enthusiastic encouragement from the Nazis and were the precursor to the later mass executions.

The Holocaust is the term used to describe the genocide of Jewish people and the killing of other groups

The persecution of the Jews continued after *Kristallnacht*. Here Jewish women are having their heads shaved and are forced to wear a sign which reads "I have been ostracized from the national community".

deemed inferior by the Nazis in Europe and North Africa throughout the war. To many, the Holocaust refers primarily to the Jewish genocide, of which *Kristallnacht* was the beginning. European Jews were the main target and approximately six million Jewish men, women and children were killed over five years. A further 220,000 Sinti and Roma people were also exterminated, along with millions of Russians, Slavs, homosexuals, Jehovah's Witnesses, Communists, Freemasons, Catholics and mentally and physically disabled people. Taking every minority group into account, it is estimated that between nine and eleven million people were killed during the Holocaust. This "Final Solution of the Jewish Question", as the Nazis called it, was carried out in stages, beginning with legislation to remove Jews from civil society. Later, those who had survived the ghettos and the appalling conditions on the trains used to transport them to concentration camps were selected either to work as slave labourers, or to be killed immediately in gas chambers, the fate of the majority.

Every arm of Germany's sophisticated bureaucracy was involved in sending Jews and others to the camps. The Interior Ministry and individual parishes identified those of Jewish heritage while the post office delivered deportation and other orders. Jewish property was confiscated and businesses discredited and fired all known Jewish workers. Throughout the Holocaust, meticulous records were kept. The German transport authorities ensured that those sent to the camps reached their destinations; German companies tendered to build the

A mass execution being carried out near Sniatyn by a German *sonderkommando* (special unit).

Jews in the
Drancy holding
and transfer camp
near Paris in 1941.

camp ovens, and pharmaceutical companies applied to
test drugs on the inmates. At the camps all prisoners were
forced to relinquish any personal property they had with
them and all of it was put to use. At this stage, not one
organization or institution in the world declared solidarity
with the Jews.

Throughout Nazi-occupied Europe and beyond, the degradation and slaughter of the Jews was deliberate and systematic. Those in central and eastern Europe suffered the worst, but no Jew was safe, whether in France, Belgium, Greece, Yugoslavia, or the Netherlands. Anyone with three or four Jewish grandparents was killed without exception. Some German Jews managed to convert to other religions, but this option was not available to Jews in the countries which the Nazis occupied. The worst atrocities were the experiments carried out on concentration camp inmates, most notoriously by Dr Josef Mengele at Auschwitz. Even those victims who survived

French Jews selected for deportation wait at the Hospital Rothschild in Paris, 1943.

being frozen, placed in a pressure chamber, or being forced to undergo drug trials, were killed and dissected. Children were not spared this horror. In one experiment, Mengele attempted to change the colour of children's eyes by injecting them with chemicals. He also carried out amputations and other surgery without the use of anaesthetics. These painful, enforced, and almost invariably fatal experiments were intended in many cases to provide knowledge which would aid the survival of Axis military personnel. Some experiments were carried out to develop and test drugs and treatment methods with which to heal battlefield injuries and illnesses, while others were performed in the service of Nazi racist ideology. Dr Mengele, for example, had a particular interest in experimenting on twins. Conventionally, doctors are seen as healers and the saviours of mankind, but this was far from the case in the concentration camps. Rather than caring for and healing their "patients", Nazi doctors

A roll call of Hungarian Jews at Auschwitz in 1944.

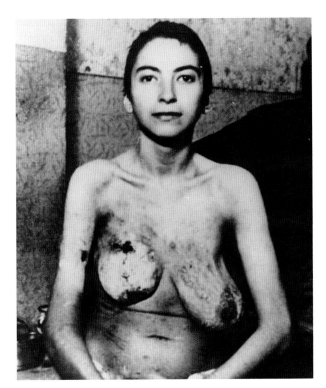

An injured survivor of medical experiments carried out at Auschwitz.

deliberately and systematically degraded their victims before taking their lives. The "Angel of Death", as Mengele was known, was responsible for heinous genetic testing. As well as experimenting on twins, whom he would meticulously examine and measure from head to toe before beginning his experiments. Mengele was also on the look-out for people who suffered from dwarfism or any other unusual physical defects. Once Mengele had collected sufficient data from each pair of twins, they would be killed by an injection of chloroform into the heart. This was done so that each twin died at exactly the same moment. Once dead, the twins would be dissected

Hungarian Jews during the notorious "selection" to determine those fit to work and those to be killed, on the platform at Auschwitz-Birkenau in June 1944.

and their organs sent to research facilities. One set of twins, aged about four, were sewn together, back to back. With their wounds infected and oozing pus, and in excruciating pain, the children were killed by their mother to end their suffering with some chloroform that she had managed to lay her hands on. Older twins, aged about eighteen, also suffered at the hands of Mengele. Two Hungarian boys, described as "extremely athletic", having been washed and examined, were X-rayed before having tubes forced up their noses and down into their lungs. A gas was then forced through the tubes forcing the twins to cough so violently that they had to be restrained. Sputum was then collected from their lungs and the twins were photographed over several days so that Mengele could examine their patterns of hair growth. Each twin would be forced to stand for hours, in great discomfort, so that the hair under their arms could be photographed. Each morning they would be woken early and made to sit in a vat of extremely hot water until they were on the point of passing out from the unbearable heat. They were then strapped to tables so that their hair could be plucked out, the idea being to save the root from each hair. They were

A pile of shoes of murdered inmates found by Soviet troops who liberated Auschwitz in January 1945.

Children from the Lodz ghetto during their deportation to Chelmno extermination camp.

Perhaps the best known account of life as a Jew under the Nazi regime is that of Anne Frank. She kept a diary for more than two years as her family hid from the authorities in occupied Amsterdam. They were eventually betrayed and Anne was sent to the Bergen-Belsen concentration camp where she died of typhus in March 1945.

Dit is een foto, zoals ik me zou wensen, altijd zo te zijn. Dan had ik nog wel een kans om naar Holywood te komen.
Annefrank.
10 Oct. 1942

(translation)
"This is a photo as I would wish myself to look all the time. Then I would maybe have a chance to come to Hollywood."
Anne Frank, 10 Oct. 1942

forced back into the hot vat several times until enough hair had been collected, following which they were shaved from head to toe. Both boys were then subjected to painful rectal and extensive lower gastric intestinal examinations, having received no anaesthetic, before receiving equally excruciating urological examinations. After three weeks of this kind of treatment, the twins were taken to the dissection laboratory where they were killed with injections into their hearts. Their bodies were then dissected and their organs sent to a research laboratory.

Other experiments were equally gruesome. Freezing and hypothermia experiments were carried out on male prisoners in order to gauge how German troops on the Eastern Front could better cope with the extremely harsh conditions in which they were fighting, for which they were ill-equipped. Thousands of troops died from hypothermia or were forced out of action by their debilitating injuries as a result of the bitterly cold conditions. Carried out at Birkenau, Dachau and

Auschwitz by Dr Sigmund Rascher, who reported directly to Himmler, the experiments were ordered by the Nazi High Command.

Inmates would be frozen to the point of death and then experiments would be performed on the best way to resuscitate them. Victims would be either forced into an icy vat of water or stripped naked and left outside in sub-zero temperatures strapped to a stretcher. The icy vat proved to be the quicker way to freeze prisoners, each of whom was stripped naked before having an insulated probe inserted in his or her rectum. On average, victims died when their body temperature dropped to around 25 degrees Celsius, having first lost consciousness.

Resuscitation proved no less painful. Victims were either placed under sun lamps so hot they burned the skin, or had blisteringly hot water forced into their stomachs, bladders, and intestines through irrigation, a method which usually resulted in death. Other resuscitation methods included placing the victim in a warm bath and slowly raising the temperature. If this was done too quickly, however, the victim died. Rascher also devised a fourth method of resuscitation on the instructions of Himmler: women were forced to have sexual intercourse with victims, a method which had some degree of success.

Creating a perfect Nordic or Aryan Race was fundamental to the Nazi ideal, so genetic experiments were performed in pursuit of this goal. Blond hair and blue eyes were a a prime requirement. Those who did not meet certain criteria were to be eliminated from society by genocide. Experiments were conducted to refine the "master race" and to determine the causes of any defects. Some prisoners were sterilized in experiments aimed at determining the best way to perform the mass sterilization of Jews and other groups. Various techniques, making use of X-rays, surgery and drugs were used. Some of the chemicals injected into victims had side effects such as internal bleeding and abdominal pain. Victims were not told what was being done to them, or why. Shortly after filling out a form they would find themselves subjected to radiation or toxic chemicals. Radiation was found to be an effective form of sterilization, though those experimented on suffered terrible burns.

Other experiments had military implications. In Dachau, doctors conducted high-altitude experiments by using a low-pressure chamber to determine at what altitude German pilots and crew could safely parachute from their aircraft, while in Ravensbrück, bone-grafting experiments were carried out. In Natzweiler and Sachsenhausen, prisoners were deliberately injured and exposed to phosgene and mustard gas so that doctors could experiment with different antidotes. Investigations into various forms of poisons and their effects were carried out on inmates. Some had poisons administered via their food, while others were shot with poisonous bullets, both methods resulting in excruciating pain. In other cases, victims were killed immediately after poison had been administered so that autopsies could take place immediately.

When the barbaric acts of the "doctors" in the camps came to light following the Holocaust the world at large was shocked. While many of the doctors and their staff escaped punishment in the so-called "Doctors Trial" at Nuremberg, and lived out their lives unhindered after the war, some of those responsible were later hunted, and, in

A female prisoner facing execution in Belzec camp, Poland.

some cases, found, by Jewish organizations seeking justice.

The largest concentration and extermination camp was Auschwitz, located about 286 kilometres from Warsaw and fifty kilometres west of Krakow in Poland. The camp commander, who reported directly to Himmler's SS was Rudolf Hoess. Auschwitz I, the site of the original camp was the administrative centre, while Auschwitz II, also known as Birkenau, was developed later as a purpose-built extermination camp, while a third, Monowitz, was a work camp. Those who were sent to Birkenau, ninety per cent of them European Jews, were killed almost immediately with the use of Zyklon B gas. Of those not killed immediately, many soon died from forced labour, starvation, disease, execution, and medical experiments.

Auschwitz I was established in May 1940 on the site of a former Polish army barracks. A month later it received its first inmates, 728 Polish prisoners. Initially it was used to detain intellectuals, resistance members, Soviet POWs, and homosexuals, forty-eight of whom were interned there at one stage. Once Jews began to be sent to Auschwitz, at any one time it would house around 13,000 to 16,000 prisoners. Different categories of prisoners were distinguished from each other by marks on their clothes. German prisoners, for example, enjoyed certain privileges in return for which they were expected to supervise other prisoners and help to maintain order – such prisoners were known as *kapos*. Jews, on the other hand, were singled out for treatment even harsher than that meted out to other inmates.

The work was backbreaking and the punishments for infractions cruel. Inmates who broke a rule might be punished by being forced into "standing cells," four to a room no bigger than one and a half metres square. Having been compelled to spend all night on their feet, the inmates would then have to return to work the next day. There were also starvation cells in which prisoners were

Prisoners at Dachau concentration camp doing forced labour in 1943.

deprived of food and water and simply left to die, and alongside the starvation cells, in the basement of the punishment block, were the so-called "dark cells." Each one was fitted with a solid door and only a tiny window. Prisoners held in these cells would slowly suffocate as they used up the available oxygen. SS guards would also often light candles to use up the oxygen more quickly. Prisoners would also be hung from their wrists with their hands behind their backs in an excruciatingly painful position intended to dislocate the shoulders. Some inmates were left like this for hours, or even days.

Executions were carried out at Auschwitz in a yard specifically designed for the purpose. Prisoners were either shot, or suspended from hooks. Then, in 1941, the

Bodies of prisoners lie in the snow at Auschwitz.

Prisoners pull Hans Bonarevitz on a handcart to his execution at Mauthausen concentration camp in July 1942. Prisoners who attempted to escape were often led to their execution by a band, often playing the light-hearted melody "All The Little Birds Are Already Here."

The entrance to Theresienstadt camp. The lettering above the gate reads "Work Brings Freedom".

first poison gas tests were carried out using cyanide. More than 800 Poles and 600 Soviet POWs were killed in the first experiment with gas on 3 September. The gas used, Zyklon B, proved to be successful on a massive scale and a bunker was specially converted so that more exterminations could be carried out in this way. An enormous crematorium was built next door in which to burn the victims' bodies. Some prisoners were selected to join *sonderkommandos* (special units) to run the gas chamber and to work in the crematorium. Part of their job was to ensure that victims undressed and kept moving into the gas chamber. Once the victims were dead, the *sonderkommandos* were responsible for removing the bodies from the chambers and taking them to the large furnaces. In March 1942, the first women prisoners were taken to Auschwitz, and the first sterilization experiments were carried out, in many cases involving the injection of caustic chemicals directly into the uterus. A painful death was the usual result, either shortly after or while the victim was being experimented on. As well as performing genetic experiments, Mengele also carried out castrations without anaesthetic.

At this time, the main camp was becoming crowded and more accommodation was needed so Auschwitz II, or Birkenau, was built. The effectiveness of gas chambers had been proved and it was decided that Auschwitz II would become the main extermination centre, as well as providing more accommodation for ever greater numbers of prisoners. There were four gas chambers in Birkenau, each one considerably larger than the original chamber. They were designed to look like enormous shower rooms in order to deceive unsuspecting new arrivals into being co-operative. By now, prisoners were arriving at Auschwitz on a daily basis by freight train. New arrivals would be divided into four different groups. The first, usually about three quarters of each group of new arrivals, were destined for the gas chambers more or less immediately. This group included all children and women with children, the elderly, and anyone who appeared unfit. More than 20,000 people could be murdered and their bodies burned in a single day. In fact, the highest figure for a single day was 24,000.

The second group comprised those who appeared fit enough to work. Between the camp's opening and its liberation in 1945, it is estimated that 400,000 people worked as slave labourers. Some Jewish workers were saved by German industrialist Oskar Schindler. Although a member of the Nazi Party, Schindler attempted to save as many Jews as he could. He called his Jewish workers "his children" and was instrumental in saving the lives of more than 1,100 Polish Jews, who would otherwise almost certainly have died in Auschwitz. He did this by convincing the SS that the workers were indispensable to his factory.

People in the third group were destined to be experimented on by Dr Josef Mengele. This group comprised twins, anyone with dwarfism, and anyone with an unusual physical appearance. Their fate was to experience excruciating pain while being experimented on before being killed.

The fourth group comprised women who were made to work in what was known as "Canada," the building in Birkenau in which the belongings of dead inmates were sorted. The building was called "Canada" because Poles who had gone to Canada were renowned for sending back exquisite and expensive gifts.

Despite the terrible conditions and great danger in Auschwitz where violating any rule or regulation meant certain death, there was some resistance within the camp. By 1943 a movement had developed which succeeded in helping a few prisoners to escape. One of those brave escapees was the scientist, Rudolf Vrba, who was able to tell the world what was really happening in the concentration camps as opposed to the misinformation disseminated by the Nazis. At Theresienstadt concentration camp (also known as Terezin) which was located in what is now the Czech Republic, the Nazis allowed the Red Cross to visit in 1944 in order to dispel rumours of extermination camps. But things were carefully arranged to deceive the visitors.

Terezin was terribly overcrowded, so, before the Red Cross visit, many of the inmates were transferred to Auschwitz. To convince the Red Cross delegation, which was led by E Juel-Henningsen, the head doctor at the Danish Ministry of Health, and Franz Hvass, an official in the Danish Foreign Ministry, that the Jews in Terezin were being well treated, fake shops and cafés were erected in the camp. The cells were given a fresh coat of paint and there were no more than three inmates to a room.

The Red Cross delegation was also treated to a performance of a children's opera, *Brundibár*, composed by Hans Krasa, an inmate of the camp. Krasa had originally written the opera for a competition held by the Czech government, but political unrest had caused the event to be cancelled. The opera was first performed by children living in an orphanage in Prague which had become a temporary school for children who had become separated from their parents because of the war. Krasa and many of the children in the orphanage were later transported to the camp where they were reunited. The Czech composer reworked the opera to make use of the instruments available in the camp and it had been performed fifty-five times before the special performance for the Red Cross delegation. Krasa was later executed in Auschwitz.

With the prisoners having been coerced into playing along with the Nazi ruse, the Red Cross delegation was completely hoodwinked into believing that life in the camps was exactly as the Nazis had portrayed it. Indeed, so successful was the hoax that the Nazis began production of a propaganda film that same year. Devised as a way to show how well the Jews were being treated under the Nazis, the film was directed by Kurt Gerron, a former director and actor who had appeared with Marlene Dietrich in *The Blue Angel*. Gerron was himself a prisoner who was transported, along with most of the rest of the cast, to Auschwitz as soon as the film had been completed.

Dachau, established by the National Socialist German Workers Party on 22 March 1933, was the first concentration camp to open, and served as a model for all subsequent concentration camps. It was divided into two parts, one of which contained its thirty-two barracks, and another which housed the crematorium. One barracks housed clergy who had opposed the Nazi regime, including bishops, deacons and priests – it is estimated that around 3,000 religious prisoners were held there. Another was used for experiments on prisoners. A large courtyard served as an area for executions. Between 1937 and 1938, prisoners were forced to rebuild the camp, after which it remained largely unchanged until its liberation on 29 April 1945. The camp was consistently overcrowded and conditions were particularly inhumane.

Although the camp had no gas chambers, conditions at Bergen-Belsen concentration camp were so appalling that the average life expectancy of inmates was only about nine months. Terrible overcrowding meant that many inmates succumbed to disease, including the young diarist Anne Frank who died there in March 1945, of typhus, just a few weeks before the camp was liberated by the British Army.

The furnace at Bergen-Belsen used to cremate bodies.

By mid-1944 the Nazi's "final solution" had gone a long way towards achieving its objective with many Jewish communities having been exterminated. Majdanek was liberated by the Red Army in July that year, and Auschwitz six months later, in January 1945. US troops liberated Buchenwald in April and the British arrived at Bergen-Belsen the same month. Dachau was liberated by US troops, in April, on the same day that Soviet forces liberated Ravensbrück. The Allied liberators struggled to comprehend what they found. Many inmates had long since died, either executed or from exhaustion, hunger, and disease. Corpses lay unburied and those who had survived were malnourished and ill.

There is no generally agreed, precise figure for how many people died in the Nazi death camps. The figure of six million Jewish victims is often quoted, but the total number of victims was substantially higher than this. The following estimates of the numbers of people who died have been made for the various camps:

Auschwitz	1,100,000
Belzec	600,000
Bergen-Belsen	35,000
Chelmno	320,000
Dachau	32,000
Gross-Rosen	40,000
Koldichevo	22,000
Majdanek	360,000
Mauthausen	120,000
Natzweiler/Struthof	12,000
Neuengamme	56,000
Plaszow	8,000
Sobibor	250,000
Stutthof	65,000
Theresienstadt	33,000
Total	3,053,000

The skulls of murdered prisoners are displayed following the liberation of Majdanek camp near Lublin, Poland, by units of the 1st White Russian Front on 24 July 1944.

Chapter 10

The defeat of Nazi Germany

As far back as 1943, there were signs that Nazi Germany was beginning to lose its grip on the war. Hitler had clearly underestimated the resilience of the Soviet Union, which , partly through sheer weight of numbers, had begun to push the German Army back and ultimately out of Soviet territory. The Germans had come tantalizingly close to capturing Moscow, but had not quite managed to breach Soviet defences. Hitler had also critically misjudged the situation in North Africa; had Rommel been allowed sufficient troops and equipment, he may well have succeeded in capturing Egypt and the oilfields beyond, but Hitler's focus on the Soviet Union had led to Rommel

There were factions within Germany which thought the country would be better off without Hitler. This is the scene of an assassination attempt on 20 July 1944 near Rastenburg – Goering and Bormann view the destruction.

D-Day: the beginning of the end for the Third Reich as Allied troops land in Normandy.

Reinforcements arrive on Omaha Beach, Normandy.

being forced out of Africa altogether. Hitler had also calculated that the United States would be completely occupied by its war in the east and unable to contribute its industrial might to the attack on occupied Europe, but its contribution of men and material was to prove overwhelming for Nazi Germany.

On 6 June 1944, D-Day, Allied landings involving mainly British, US, and Canadian forces began on the coast of Normandy in France. The invasion force was augmented by troops from France, Poland, Belgium,

Greece, Czechoslovakia, Norway and Holland, with additional naval and air support from a number of other allied nations. The invasion of German-occupied Europe began with attacks by paratroopers, some of whom landed in gliders, supported by a naval bombardment and waves of air attacks in advance of the amphibious landings. The Germans had anticipated that the Allies would invade, but they did not know exactly where, nor when. They had been misled to believe that the Allies would land at Pas-de-Calais at the point closest to England, which would have maximised the flying time available to Spitfire and Hawker Typhoon fighter planes flying in support of naval and ground forces.

The Germans also thought that the bad weather which had been forecast would delay the attack. On both counts they were to be proved wrong. The Allies had been deterred from attacking Pas-de-Calais by its strong fortifications which it was felt would cost too many lives. Eisenhower had tentatively chosen 5 June as the date for the assault, but the weather conditions – high seas and

A German coastal battery attempts to repel the Allied invasion forces.

strong winds – were unsuitable for an amphibious landing; it would be impossible to launch the landing craft, and low clouds would hamper close air support. However, at a critical meeting which took place on 5 June, Eisenhower's chief meteorologist, Group Captain J M Stagg forecast a brief spell of better weather for the following day.

Eisenhower seized this brief window of opportunity and gave the order for the assault to go ahead. When it came, on the beaches of Normandy, to the west of Pas-de-Calais, the Germans were taken by surprise. The assault on Sword Beach, as it had been dubbed, began at 3.00 am with an aerial bombardment of German artillery and coastal defences. By 7.30 am, the first Allied units had landed on the beach. These were the Duplex Drive (DD) amphibious tanks of the 13th/18th Hussars which were closely followed by the 8th Infantry Brigade.

American soldiers take on a German tank in a French village as the Allies advance.

In Ouistreham, to the east of Sword Beach, British and French troops from Number 4 Commando had been given separate objectives. The French were to deal with a blockhouse and defenders in the casino, while the British were to take out two batteries overlooking the beach. The blockhouse proved resistant to the PIAT (Projector Infantry Anti-Tank) weapons being used by the French, but the casino was taken with the help of a Centaur tank. The British commandos seized both their objectives only to discover that the gun mounts were empty, the guns having been removed. The infantry followed along behind, mopping up, enabling the commandos to leave Ouistreham and move inland to link up with Numbers 3, 6, and 45 Commandos of their brigade before joining the 6th Airborne Division.

Meanwhile, on Juno Beach, the first wave of Canadian attackers suffered fifty per cent casualties as they confronted eleven batteries of 155-mm guns, nine batteries of 75-mm guns, concrete fortifications, pillboxes and machine-gun nests. The Canadian use of armour, however, proved a success, landing ahead of the infantry and helping to clear a path inland. In spite of their losses and the obstacles which they faced, the Canadians were off the beach within hours and were the only Allied troops to achieve their D-Day objective, when both the 6th Canadian Armoured Regiment (1st Hussars) and the Queen's Own Rifles of Canada had crossed the Caen-Bayeux highway, nine miles inland.

By the end of the day, 15,000 Canadian troops had been successfully landed and the 3rd Canadian Infantry Division had penetrated further into France than any other Allied force. This was accomplished in spite of fierce resistance from elements of the 21st and 12th SS *Hitlerjugend* Panzer divisions on 7 and 8 June.

There were also heavy casualties on Gold Beach due, in part, to the Germans having created a heavily fortified village on the beach and because of the delayed arrival of Sherman DD tanks. Nevertheless, the 50th (Northumbrian) Infantry Division had almost reached the outskirts of Bayeux by the end of the day and, apart from the Canadians, came closest to achieving all its objectives that day. Also on Gold Beach, Number 47 (Royal Marine) Commando was the last British commando unit to land, just east of Le Hamel, from where they made their way ten miles west through enemy territory to launch an attack from behind on the harbour of Port-en-Bessin.

Omaha Beach would forever be dubbed "Bloody Omaha" as it suffered the largest number of casualties, around 3,000, all of whom were American. Nothing really went according to plan during the assault. Even before the landing, ten landing craft and the soldiers in them were lost when they were swamped by high seas. Furthermore, the soldiers, drawn from the 1st and 29th Infantry Divisions, had received intelligence that they would be coming up against the relatively poor quality German 716th Division, only to be confronted by the highly experienced veterans of the 352nd Division, one of the best trained German forces defending any beach.

Omaha also proved to be the most heavily fortified beach and, for the most part, both aerial and naval bombardments prior to the landings had been relatively ineffective. This resulted in American troops being wounded or killed before they could even disembark from their landing crafts and only two of thirty-four Sherman

In June 1944, the Germans unleashed their new V-1 (*Vergeltungswaffe*- or "Vengeance weapon"-1) pilotless flying bombs against targets in the south-east of England and Belgium. They were known popularly as "buzz bombs" or "doodlebugs" because of the characteristic noise made by their simple pulse jet engines.

tanks made it ashore. At one stage, US commanders considered abandoning the beachhead, given the tremendous number of casualties that had been suffered and the fact that it was almost impossible to land any further craft due to all the wreckage, fires and casualties which covered the beach. In the end, it was left to small, isolated pockets of infantrymen supported by naval artillery and any surviving tanks to infiltrate the coastal defences by scaling the bluffs between the German strongholds.

Off Utah Beach, the 4th Infantry Division landing force found itself swept off course by unexpectedly powerful currents, though this proved to be a blessing in disguise as they eventually came ashore in Victor Sector, which was

As the Allies battled their way inland from the Normandy beaches, the French resistance stepped up their fight against the German occupiers.

only lightly defended, so they encountered minimal resistance. In fact, they suffered only 200 casualties out of 23,000 troops, the lightest number of casualties on any beach during the Normandy landings.

By 13 June, the Allies had succeeded in linking all the beaches and were reinforcing more rapidly than the Germans were able to replenish their own forces. The cost to the Allies in casualties of the Normandy landings was high, but the successful establishment of a beachhead was a critical step in the ultimate defeat of Germany. In the aftermath of the Normandy landings, it was clear that the strategy adopted by the combined Allied forces, devised largely by British and US staff officers, had outmanoeuvred the Germans, despite the fierce defence which they put up. Allied intelligence and counter-intelligence had obviously achieved more than had been hoped for, and Allied air support, too, played a crucial role in the success of the landings. Not only did the landings damage German military capacity and morale, they also enabled large numbers of men and great quantities of equipment to be brought ashore, both of which were to prove crucial in the weeks and months to come. In less than two weeks following D-Day, 630,000 troops, 95,000 vehicles and 116,000 tons of supplies had been brought ashore. As the Allies moved inshore, 9,000 tons of supplies a day continued to be landed at Arromanches harbour until the end of August 1944, by which time the port of Cherbourg had been secured and was available for use by Allied shipping.

Parisians celebrate the liberation of their city on 25 August 1944.

Following the landings, the Allies had momentum and morale was high. The success of the landings also boosted Soviet morale, as they had been battling alone in the east against the overwhelming bulk of Hitler's forces for years; Allied success in the west had a tremendous impact on their own advance. Although the terrain over which the Allies had to advance to Germany would, all other things being equal, have favoured Germany, the Allies by now had great superiority in troop numbers, armoured vehicles, and planes. However, those Germans still in the field were in no mood to surrender just yet. In spite of the failed attempt to assassinate Hitler with a bomb during a meeting, carried out earlier in the year by disillusioned members of the German military, on 16 December 1944 the Germans launched a counteroffensive in the Ardennes.

German soldiers surrender in Paris, August 1944.

Dubbed *Unternehmen: Wacht am Rhein* (Operation Watch on the Rhine), the resulting battle is commonly referred to as the Battle of the Bulge. The Germans aimed to split the British and US line in two, capturing the Belgian city of Antwerp in the process, then to encircle and destroy the four Allied armies. If they could achieve this, they anticipated that the Western Allies would have no option but to negotiate a peace treaty which would favour Germany, Italy, and Japan. The German plan was shrouded in secrecy to the extent that the Allies were largely deprived of radio intelligence. While not completely unexpected, when it came the German attack still took the Allies by surprise. The Battle of the Bulge was the bloodiest battle fought by US forces during the Second World War, with over 19,000 killed in three regiments of

A German panzer advances during the Battle of the Bulge, leaving a destroyed US tank in its wake.

the US 106th Infantry Division. Poor weather hampered efforts to help the embattled US forces, who were largely dependent on air support. It was not until 23 December

Soviet bombers above the Reichstag and Soviet tanks enter Berlin in April 1945.

that the Allies were able to launch a series of devastating attacks against the Germans. With the Luftwaffe severely weakened following the Normandy landings, the Allies were able to recapture the initiative. However, the Luftwaffe was still able to launch one last, big raid, on New Year's Day, 1945, when it destroyed or damaged over 460 Allied aircraft.

Less than a week later, though, on 7 January, Hitler was forced to announce that he was withdrawing all German forces from the Ardennes, including the SS Panzer divisions, thereby signalling the end of German offensive operations. But the war was still far from won, and the Allies faced a hard fight to the German border and beyond. Having liberated France and the Low Countries, the Allies succeeded in forcing German forces back across the border into Germany, while on Germany's eastern borders the Russian juggernaut continued to gain momentum. Having driven the Nazis out of the Soviet Union the year before, Russian troops were advancing on Berlin, the battle for which was to be one of the last of the war. In the so-called Berlin Offensive Operation, two enormous Soviet army groups attacked Berlin from the east and from the south, while a third unit pulverized German forces to the north of the city. The Allies, who had met up with Soviet troops for the first time on the River Elbe, did not play a role in the battle for Berlin. Eisenhower had expressed the view that further Allied casualties would be wasted as the Soviets were to be responsible for governing Berlin in the immediate aftermath of the war.

The Battle of the Seelow Heights, the final German defensive position keeping Soviet forces from the centre of Berlin, was fought over four days from 16 to 19 April. It

Soviet soldiers in front of the bodies of Nazis who have committed suicide in a Viennese park in April 1945.

involved almost a million Soviet troops and more than 20,000 tanks and artillery, far outnumbering Germany's 100,000 troops and 1,200 tanks and artillery. As Soviet forces advanced on the city itself, the fighting became increasingly bloody hand-to-hand combat from house to house. SS remnants fought most tenaciously, partly out of ideological belief, partly because they felt that they were unlikely to survive for long if captured.

On 30 April, Soviet troops finally captured the ruined Reichstag, Germany's final humiliation. Hitler signed his will that day as well as married his lover Eva Braun, but there would be no honeymoon. Shortly after the ceremony, held in Hitler's bunker, they both took cyanide, which had been given to Hitler's dog earlier that day in order to test it, and then Hitler shot himself. It is thought that Eva died from the poison alone.

By the end of the day, the Soviet flag would be flying from the top of the Reichstag, and the war in Europe would be over, bar the formalities of surrender. On 1 May, German forces in Italy surrendered, followed, on 4 May, by those in north-west Germany, Holland and Denmark. Hitler's will had appointed Admiral Karl Dönitz as the new president of Germany and on 6 May, Dönitz authorized General Jodl to announce the complete and total surrender of all German forces. At precisely 2.41 am, on the morning of 7 May 1945 at the Supreme Headquarters Allied Expeditionary Force in Rheims, the surrender document was formally signed by Jodl. It included the phrase: "All forces under German control to cease active operations at 23.01 hours Central European Time on 8 May 1945."

Soviet soldiers in front of the former Reich Chancellery surround the body of a civilian, who was mistaken for Hitler and shot dead.

By May 1945 the
Third Reich lay in
ruins.

On 8 May itself, General Wilhelm Keitel and other German representatives traveled to a villa in the town of Karhorst, just outside Berlin to meet with the Soviet General Georgi Zhukov, in order to sign a document surrendering to the Soviet forces. The news of this unconditional surrender spread through Europe and the United States on 8 May and celebrations erupted on what came to be known as V-E Day, Victory in Europe Day. Because the Soviet surrender agreement was not formalized until shortly before midnight, Russia and other eastern European countries celebrate V-E Day on 9 May.

After six long years of Nazi terror, the celebrations continued for quite some time. However, the full extent of

Adolf Hitler's will, signed on 29 April 1945, which announced his and his new wife's suicide.

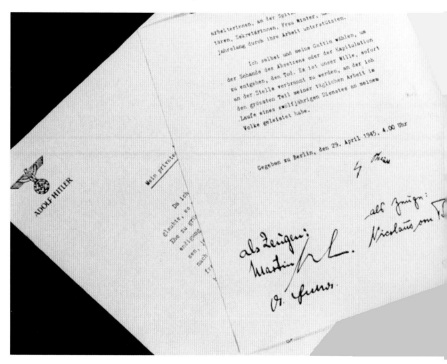

the brutality of the Nazi regime was only just beginning to come to light in some quarters. As war-weary Europeans celebrated, the Nazi legacy was revealed as, one by one, the concentration camps were liberated. In April 1945, as the British Army advanced across Lower Saxony towards the Aller River, the Germans initiated negotiations to surrender the nearby Bergen–Belsen concentration camp. They claimed that their motive for doing this was that the camp contained 9,000 sick inmates, many of whom had

A British sentry in Bremen outside a shop offering *Wehrmacht* and police hats for sale.

typhus, but that they had no water or medical supplies with which to treat them. They did not wish, they claimed, the epidemic to spread further and contaminate the soldiers. When the British finally took control of the camp on 15 April, they were met by several hundred emaciated inmates whose ribs protruded and whose bellies were distended. Such was their physical condition and psychological state that many simply sat and stared at their liberators, unaware that their nightmare was coming to an end. In Number 1 camp, the inmates had suffered the most. Over the preceding weeks, 60,000, prisoners, most of them Jewish, had been brought to Bergen-Belsen from other concentration camps in the face of the Allied advance. Through overcrowding they experienced horrendous conditions and many prisoners died as a result of dehydration, starvation, and inadequate shelter. When

Auschwitz concentration camp is liberated by Soviet forces.

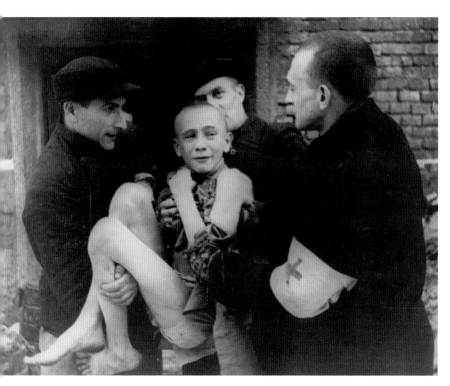

British forces liberated Number 1 camp, they discovered 20,000 naked corpses unburied, victims who had been too weak to crawl away from the typhus-ridden corpses which surrounded them.

Members of the Red Cross carry fifteen-year-old Ivan Dudnik out of Auschwitz.

British troops later recalled that the stench of rotting human flesh could still be detected over three miles away from the camp. Initially, the water supply had been cut off after an Allied bombing raid. There was a creek nearby which the Nazi guards had used to collect water for their own use, however no water was made available to the thousands of prisoners, most of whom died within six days as a result of dehydration.

Members of the
SS surrender.

One of the most important tasks faced by the liberators was to meet the medical needs of the survivors. At Bergen-Belsen alone, British doctors estimated that 20,000 of the approximately 50,000 survivors were in either a serious or a critical condition and in need of urgent medical assistance.

It was largely through a process of trial and error that medical staff were able to develop special foods which were both nutritious and sufficiently easily digestible for the very ill prisoners. These relief efforts made enormous psychological demands on the British forces as they dealt with a situation for which they had not been trained and for which, despite their battlefield experiences, they were thoroughly unprepared. Partly in order to spare British troops further psychological trauma, German and Hungarian SS former guards were made to carry the bodies to mass graves which had been dug by British Army bulldozers. As the weeks passed, the British were slowly, but surely able to rehouse all the prisoners who had regained sufficient health in local houses commandeered from German civilians. Finally, when the last inmates were able to leave, the British burned down the camp to prevent the lice, which spread typhus, from causing further harm.

Despite the tremendous efforts made by troops who liberated concentration camps, many inmates were simply too weak and ill to survive. In Bergen-Belsen alone, 13,000 of those inmates who had survived the war died following liberation. Destroying the camp by fire to prevent the further spread of typhus also destroyed a reminder of the horror of the camps; a potential memorial of man's inhumanity towards man was lost.

The bodies of prisoners in Bergen-Belsen concentration camp after its liberation by British forces in the spring of 1945.

A US soldier examines a gas chamber disguised as a shower after the liberation of Dachau concentration camp.

When Dachau was liberated by US troops on 29 April 1945, what they found defied belief. In each of twenty barracks, designed to hold up to 250 people, they found 1,600 inmates crowded together – a total of 32,000 prisoners in the camp as a whole. They also discovered approximately forty railway cars, each one filled with a hundred or more corpses. That day, 520 Germans were killed by US troops and inmates, the vast majority of them machine-gunned by US troops once they had surrendered.

Similar stories of Nazi brutality emerged with the liberation of the other twenty or so concentration camps, such as Buchenwald and Flössenburg, and additional forced labour camps. When accounts from the different camps began to reach the outside world, they left an indelible impression on Western public opinion which has lasted to this day. The photographs, newsreel footage and Hollywood dramatizations have kept alive the power of this period of history to affect people, including leaders

and decision-makers, ever since. The carnage inflicted by the Nazis has led to widespread and intense revulsion at what they stood for. In 1945, as the horrors of their rule became known, celebrations of new-found freedom and hope for a better future were marred by sadness and horror as more graphic details began to emerge of the full extent of the destruction and terror of Nazi rule. The images that appeared in newspapers and newsreels roused in the people of all nations who had suffered at the hands of the Nazis a clamour for justice which would culminate in the Nuremberg War Crimes Trials.

Survivors at Bergen-Belsen concentration camp.

Chapter 11

Nuremberg and the aftermath

The Nuremberg Trials, the first international war crimes trials to be held, took place between 1945 and 1949. The choice of Nuremberg as a venue was significant as it was there that the Nazi Party had held its annual rallies. There were twelve trials in total, but it was the first which really captured the attention of the public as it focused on the twenty-one most notorious Nazis. What really gripped the imagination of the public, once the trials had begun and people could begin to put faces to names when reading newspaper reports, was how ordinary these "terrorists" appeared to be. Many defendants appeared to be unassuming, family-oriented men, yet they had ordered the killing of thousands upon thousands of ordinary civilians, just like them, and caused, directly or indirectly, the death of millions more.

Prior to the Nuremberg trials, there had been much debate among the leading politicians of the Allied countries as to how the perpetrators of such atrocities should be dealt with. Some preferred an "eye-for-an-eye" approach, whereby the defendants should be made to pay for their crimes by being executed themselves. Others suggested that those found guilty should be made responsible for the rebuilding of Europe. Then there were those who advocated destroying what remained of Germany's industrial base to weaken it to the extent that it

Rudolph Hoess
after his arrest in
Gottrupel near
Flensburg.

would never again be able to wage war, and would have to rely primarily on agriculture.

In the end, however, it was agreed that the perpetrators would stand trial in Nuremberg. Representing the prosecution were Robert H Jackson (for the United States), Sir Hartley Shawcross (UK), Lieutenant-General R A Rudenko (Soviet Union), and François de Menthon and Auguste Champetier de Ribes (France).

Herman Goering takes the witness stand at the Nuremberg Trials.

The indictments brought against the accused were:

- Participation in a common plan or conspiracy for the accomplishment of crime against peace – this addressed crimes committed before the war had begun.

- War crimes – this addressed more traditional violations of the law with regard to the mistreatment and killing of prisoners of war and the use of banned weapons.

- Crimes against humanity – this addressed crimes committed against Jews and other ethnic minorities as well as crimes against the mentally and physically disabled.

- Planning, initiating, and waging wars of aggression and other crimes against peace – this addressed the undertaking of war in violation of international treaties and assurances.

Of course, Adolf Hitler and Joseph Goebbels, the Minister for Public Enlightenment and Propaganda, had already committed suicide, and Martin Bormann, the Nazi Party Secretary, had gone missing. All three would otherwise certainly have appeared as defendants in the trial. However, high-profile Nazis who did stand trial included Rudolf Hoess, Hermann Goering, Alfred Jodl, Wilhelm Keitel, Hans Frank and Karl Dönitz.

The trial opened on 20 November 1945 and began with the reading of the indictments. Obviously, the greatest Nazi crime had been the systematic murder of Jews throughout occupied Europe. For an entire day, the defendants were forced to listen as the prosecution read out the detailed list of crimes they stood accused of having committed.

The trial of the major war criminals before the International Military Tribunal in the Palace of Justice in Nuremberg, 1945. Front row, from left: Goering, Hoess, von Ribbentrop, Keitel, Kaltenbrunner, Streicher, Frank, Schacht. Back row, from left: Doenitz, Raeder, Schirach, Sauckel, Jodel, von Papen, Seyss-Inquart, Speer, von Neurath, Fritsche.

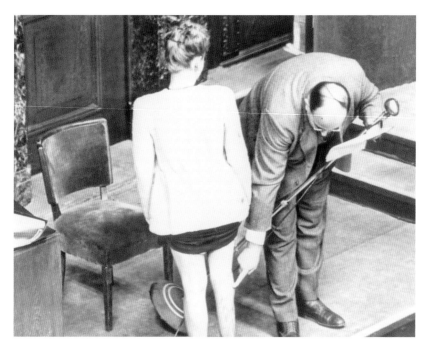

A demonstration of the results of medical experiments on Polish student J Dzido, a former prisoner at the Ravensbrück concentration camp.

On the following day, Robert Jackson delivered his opening statement for the prosecution. Its case would be split into two distinct phases. The first phase was focused on trying to establish the criminality of the various components of the Nazi regime and to establish the guilt of specific individuals. The second phase concerned the concentration camps and the Nazis' use of slave labour.

Sworn affidavits stated that many people held in concentration camps had had so-called "experiments" conducted on them. The Soviets showed some German footage they had captured, showing Nazi atrocities in the Soviet Union. Many of those who stood trial claimed that they knew nothing about the existence of any concentration camps. Goering was singularly unrepentant, but he could do little more than admit the truth under Jackson's severe cross-examination. Over subsequent months, the rest of the accused faced questions about their own involvement. In Jackson's closing argument on 26 July 1946, he denounced each of the defendants in turn, but his most vehement attacks were reserved for Goering. In an act of defiance, as each of the accusations were made by Jackson, Goering perversely kept count of them. In the final stage of the protracted trial, each defendant made a statement. Goering told the court that the trial had been little more than a display of power by the victors, and that "justice" had had nothing to do with it. And, while some of the defendants offered some form of superficial apology, Goering remained defiant and unrepentant.

On 1 October 1946, the twenty-one defendants filed into court for the last time for the delivery of the verdicts. The British judge, Sir Geoffrey Lawrence, began with Goering. He stated that, apart from Hitler himself, Goering had been the prime motivator for waging aggressive war,

Sentries were posted at the door of each defendant's cell in Nuremberg town prison.

that there was "nothing to be said in mitigation", that his guilt was "unique in its enormity" and that the record disclosed no excuses for him. When, in the afternoon, sentences were passed, Goering received his verdict first with Sir Geoffrey Lawrence announcing that, "The International Military Tribunal sentences you to death by hanging." Expressionless, Goering turned and left the courtroom to return to his prison cell in Nuremberg to consider an appeal, but somehow he had managed to get hold of a cyanide capsule, which he used to commit suicide the night before he was due to be executed. Ten other defendants were also sentenced to death by hanging, but others were sentenced either to life imprisonment or to prison sentences ranging from ten to twenty years, while three were acquitted.

A display board on the wall of the courtroom shows the location of the concentration camps.

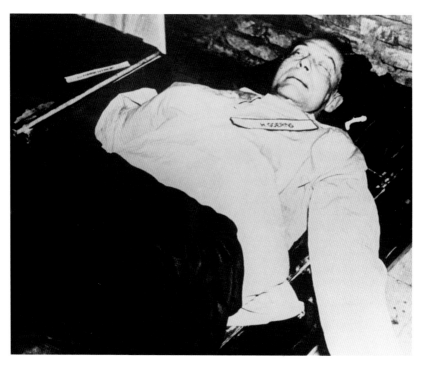

The Nuremberg Trials were intended to serve a number of purposes. While perhaps not fulfilling all of the hopes of those who had advocated them, no one could deny that they served to provide a thorough account of Nazi war crimes and they also exposed those on trial for the monsters they were, preventing them from becoming martyrs in the eyes of the German public. The trials also helped to initiate a movement for the establishment of a permanent international criminal court and aided in the drafting of the Geneva Convention, the Universal Declaration of Human Rights and the Convention on the Abolition of the Statute of Limitations on War Crimes and Crimes Against Humanity.

The body of Herman Goering in his Nuremberg prison cell after his suicide on 15 October 1946.

Meanwhile, what remained of Nazi Germany after the war was divided up into four occupation zones which had been determined at Potsdam in July and August 1945. Each territory would be controlled by one of the Allied forces – the United States, the UK, France and the Soviet Union. The capital, Berlin, was also divided into four

There were other trials besides Nuremberg. Here, German war criminals are hanged in Kiev.

zones and was home to the Allied Control Council in spite of the fact that Berlin was located deep within the zone of the Soviet Union. The original premise was that Germany would be jointly governed by the four occupying powers, but this pact soon fragmented with the advent of the Cold War. The increased tension was such that the UK, France

Oswald Pohl appeared as a witness for the prosecution during the IG-Farben Trial (August 1947 to July 1948) but was sentenced to death himself in the subsequent Trial IV of the SS.

and the United States broke ranks with the Soviet Union and, in 1949, formed what was to become the Federal Republic of Germany, more commonly known as West Germany, while the Soviet Union formed the German Democratic Republic, colloquially known as East Germany. The Berlin Wall, built to divide East Berlin from West Berlin, was a stark, physical reminder of this split between the erstwhile allies. Built in 1961, the wall continued to divide Berlin until it was dismantled in 1989. In August 1962, an East German teenager, Peter Fechter was shot while attempting to scale the wall, and left for hours to bleed to death. That same year, fourteen-year-old Wilfried Tews was hit eight times as he attempted to swim through a canal under the wall, leaving him disabled for life. Despite having been hit in the lung, legs, collarbone and arm, Tews managed to drag himself up onto the bank on the West German side. West German border guards provided covering fire, killing a twenty-one-year-old East German border guard, and a passer-by was able to drag the boy to safety. Between 1961 and 1989, the number of people killed trying to escape to the West, according to official figures, was 125. However, the real figure is believed by some to be much higher, that at least 1,245 people, including children, were killed trying to escape, under the orders of the Communist regime, although the East German government always denied that such a policy ever existed.

Doctor Herta Oberhauser is sentenced to twenty years during the trial of Nazi doctors for carrying out medical experiments on concentration camp inmates.

On 9 November 1989, after weeks of civil unrest and
more than forty years after the end of the Second World
War, the East German government announced that
entering West Berlin would be permitted and, following
that momentous declaration, crowds of East Germans

An aerial view of
the Berlin wall
around the
Brandenburg
Gate.

climbed onto and over the wall to the Western side, where
they were greeted euphorically by West Germans. Over
subsequent weeks, parts of the wall were torn down or
chipped away by celebrating Germans on both sides.
Finally, industrial equipment was brought in to remove the

last remnants of the barrier that had caused so much controversy and unnecessary death since its construction. The fall of the Berlin Wall paved the way for German reunification which was finally ratified on 3 October 1990.

After the war, Europeans, and the rest of the world, faced the daunting problem of how to reconstruct the war-ravaged continent. It is important to note that the infrastructure of the United States had been left intact by the war, and it was enjoying the benefits of a prospering economy, while experts were predicting the social and economic collapse of Europe. In June 1947, US Secretary of State, George Marshall, put forward recommendations which, when formalized, would become known as the Marshall Plan and would be, unquestionably, one of the most successful projects of civil reconstruction of the twentieth century. In a speech made at Harvard University, future Nobel Peace Prize-winner Marshall stated, "It is logical that the United States should do whatever it is able to do to assist in the return of normal economic health in the world without which, there can be no political stability and no assured peace." He went on to state that his plans were based on the initiative of the Europeans and on their own faith in the economic future of their own individual countries and of Europe as a whole. His proposals were not directed against any country specifically, he said, but against hunger, desperation, poverty, and chaos.

Within just a few weeks of this speech, European governments, led by the UK and France, began drafting Marshall's spending plan which revolved around supplying German importers of life-sustaining goods with the hard currency which they needed. By the time the Marshall Plan came to an end in 1952, the United States had spent more than 13 billion dollars in goods and investments in financial services of which about 1.4 billion dollars was invested in rebuilding Germany from the desert of rubble to which most of it had been reduced. It was not only Germany which benefitted from this investment; the UK, France and Italy also received financial aid from the United States, but Moscow rejected such aid and forbade its Eastern European satellite states to accept capitalist help. In doing so, it set the seal on what would become the Cold War as Western Europe grew increasingly reliant on the United States.

While historians have always disagreed about the extent to which the Marshall Plan helped to generate European economic recovery following the Second World War, the intentions of the United States have always been clear. US leaders believed that only through prosperity could Western Europe become a barrier strong enough to prevent Communism from taking hold in the West. While it is generally accepted that eighty to ninety per cent of the capital formation in each of the major European economies during the Marshall Plan's first two years was the result of each country's own resources, it is also acknowledged that the plan provided a critical measure of support which helped to suppress inflation, increase essential imports and facilitate production. All of this led to increased trade and productivity which created the most sustained period of peace and prosperity in modern European history.

While the Nuremberg Trials went some way to restoring justice and the rule of law, issues such as what to do with the roughly one million people who had been displaced by the war, of whom approximately twenty per cent were Jewish, remained. In 1947, a series of bills were put before the US Congress with the aim of relaxing immigration quotas to enable some of those who had lost their homes to come to the United States, but none was passed. At the same time, the UK approached the United Nations in an attempt to resolve the issue. As a result, on 29 November 1947, the UN General Assembly adopted a plan which would divide Palestine into separate Arab and Jewish states, with Jerusalem under international control.

On 14 May 1948, the Jewish state of Israel was proclaimed and the UK began to withdraw from Palestine. Almost immediately neighbouring Arab states attacked Israel and the region has been in a state of almost constant conflict since then. In the United States, the Displaced Persons Act was finally passed in 1948. President Truman was reluctant to sign it because it placed limits on the number of Jewish displaced persons who would be

Simon Wiesenthal, pictured in 2000.

permitted to emigrate to the United States, but those limits were eventually repealed in 1950. Just a year later, Israeli authorities made a claim to the four occupying powers to obtain compensation and reimbursement for the cost of absorbing and resettling over 500,000 Holocaust survivors. Estimating that each survivor cost around 3,000 dollars to resettle, Israel claimed that Germany owed them around 1.5 billion dollars. Furthermore, although Israel stressed that no amount of additional money could ever compensate for the six billion dollars of Jewish property which had been lost, and possessions which had been stolen, an agreement was finally reached in September 1952 whereby West Germany agreed to pay Israel three billion marks over fourteen years in compensation for the slave labour and persecution of the Jews during the Holocaust and Jewish property stolen by the Nazis. West Germany also agreed to pay a further 450 million marks to the World Jewish Congress. These payments did not go directly to the Jewish victims themselves but to the State of Israel as the "heir" to those victims who had been left with no surviving family members. The money was, however, invested in improving Israel's infrastructure and played a key role in establishing the new state's economy.

Although the Nuremberg Trials achieved a great deal in bringing Nazi war criminals to justice, there were still several leading Nazis who managed to escape. This was a major irritant to Jewish survivors who had, understandably, a burning desire to see justice done to everyone who had so grievously wronged them. One of the leading proponents of the movement to achieve justice was Simon Wiesenthal. His quest began after US troops liberated Mauthausen death camp in Austria, where he was a prisoner, in May 1945. Prior to that Wiesenthal had been incarcerated in numerous other camps.

When he was freed, weighing just ninety-nine pounds, Wiesenthal dedicated himself to tracking down Nazi war criminals, saying, "There is no freedom without justice." He had soon gathered many supporters as he set about his mission of hunting down Nazis in hiding in order for them to be prosecuted. Perhaps his most famous achievement was the role he played in tracking down Adolf Eichmann, the infamous SS leader who had played such a large part in organizing the murder of Jews during the Second World War. When Eichmann was captured by Israeli agents in Argentina, in May 1960, it was an historic event. He was taken to Israel where he was charged with crimes against Jews, Poles, Gypsies, Slavs and other ethnic minorities. The crimes he was charged with ranged from illegal capture and imprisonment, the deportation of innocent people to extermination camps, mass expulsions, murder and theft of property. Following his trial, he was sentenced to death and executed at midnight on 31 May 1962. Not

Adolf Eichmann in his cell before the start of his trial. The former German industrialist – charged with deporting Jews to ghettoes and concentration camps – had escaped to Buenos Aires but was captured in 1960 and subsequently found guilty. He was hanged, his body cremated and his ashes scattered in international waters so no nation could claim his resting place.

only was this seen as justice being served on a renowned Nazi war criminal, but it also shed a whole new light on the inhumanity and brutality of the Nazi regime for a new generation of Israelis and Germans in particular, but also for anyone throughout the world born either late in the war or after its end. Simon Wiesenthal never claimed that he alone was responsible for bringing Eichmann to justice, in spite of unwarranted criticism from some quarters that he had exaggerated his role in Eichmann's capture. He always stood by his admission that no one person would be able to track down all of the missing Nazi war criminals who had escaped justice, and that his effort was a collaborative one with the help of many supporters. Wiesenthal saw himself more as a spokesperson for the six million Jews who had died during the Holocaust, during which he himself had lost eighty-nine relatives. His mission was not only to track down war criminals, but also to speak out against racism and neo-Nazism and to keep the memory of the Jews' experience during the war alive as a lesson for humanity.

As well as being instrumental in the capture of Eichmann, Wiesenthal played a role in tracking down Karl Silberbauer, an Austrian policeman whom Wiesenthal believed had been responsible for the arrest of Anne Frank. His pursuit of Silberbauer began in 1958 after a youth had told him that he did not believe in Anne Frank's existence and murder but would do so if Wiesenthal could locate the man who had arrested her. His subsequent five-year search concluded with Silberbauer's capture in 1963.

Overall, it has been claimed that Wiesenthal's mission has resulted, with the help of many others, in capturing over a thousand Nazi war criminals. In spite of all his successes, however, Wiesenthal bitterly regretted "the one that got away", Dr Josef Mengele, his prime target. During his twenty-one months at Auschwitz, Mengele took turns with the other SS doctors to meet incoming prisoners and determine who would survive – for a while at least – as a slave labourer, and who would be sent immediately to the gas chambers. While many of the SS doctors apparently hated this task, Mengele is reported to have performed it with relish.

At university in Munich, Mengele had come under the influence of Dr Ernst Rudin, who taught his students that some lives were not worth living and doctors had a responsibility to destroy such lives for the good of society as a whole. He earned a PhD for a thesis which "proved" that it was possible to determine "race" by examining the jawbone. In 1937 he was appointed as a research assistant at the Third Reich Institute for Heredity, Biology and Racial Purity and, by 1938, he had joined the SS. Assigned to the Waffen SS, its combat division, Mengele was awarded the Iron Cross First Class, Germany's highest award for bravery. Wounded and unable to return to the front line, Mengele was assigned to Auschwitz. There, his main project became to devise ways of eradicating inferior genes in order to create Hitler's "perfect race". Just days after his arrival, Mengele sent a thousand gypsies directly to the gas chambers to prevent the spread of typhus.

Immediately after the war, Mengele hid, pretending to be a farmhand, in Günzburg. He hoped to be able to resume his "research", but realized that this would be impossible and fled to Argentina on an Italian ship. He spent the next thirty years in hiding, sheltered by neo-Nazi networks in Argentina, Paraguay, and Brazil. The

international uproar over the kidnapping of Adolf Eichmann by Israeli agents from Argentina may have saved Mengele the same fate.

Mengele died in Brazil in 1979. He had been in poor health for some time and died of a stroke while swimming in the sea at Santos. He was buried in secret in Embu, a suburb of Sao Paolo, where he is supposed to have lived for the last few years of his life, under the assumed name of Wolfgang Gerhard, whose ID card Mengele had been using since 1976. Following a tip-off in 1985, the German police raided a house in Günzberg and seized books, papers and letters, all of which pointed to Mengele's grave being located in Embu and, in May that year, a body was exhumed and examined by forensic experts. His only son, Rolf, was left in no doubt that the remains were those of his father, and this was finally confirmed using DNA evidence in 1992.

German industrialist Oskar Schindler, who saved more than 1,200 Jews from deportation between 1944 and 1945, is welcomed on his arrival in Israel in May 1962.

Perhaps one of the most telling insights into the minds of such Nazi war criminals was revealed by Rolf Mengele when he was interviewed around the time his father's remains were discovered. Rolf, having never previously known who his father was, visited him in Sao Paolo in 1977 and was shocked to discover that he was completely unrepentant about his Nazi past, claiming that "he had never personally harmed anyone in his entire life."

Simon Wiesenthal was well into his nineties when he announced his retirement from the Jewish Documentation Centre in Vienna, which had been his base for hunting Nazis. In announcing his intention to retire, he said that he had found the mass murderers he had primarily been looking for, with the exception of Mengele: "I have survived them all," he said. "If there were any left, they'd be too old and weak to stand trial today. My work is done."

On 20 September 2005, when Simon Wiesenthal died in his sleep, aged ninety-six, in Vienna, it was revealed the following month, when another so-called Nazi doctor, Albert Heim, was discovered in Spain that Wiesenthal had still been working on this particular case even after he had retired.

Today, his legacy lives on. The Simon Wiesenthal Centre – with headquarters in Los Angeles and offices in New York, Toronto, Paris, Palm Beach, Buenos Aires and Jerusalem – is an international Jewish human rights organization dedicated to repairing the world one step at a time. It generates change through its Snider Social Action Institute and educates by confronting anti-Semitism, race hatred and terrorism, while promoting human rights and dignity. Standing firmly alongside Israel, it aims to defend the safety of Jews worldwide and teaches the lessons of the

Holocaust so that they may be carried on for future generations.

Now, more than sixty years since the Second World War, greater awareness of the horror of war and the particularly barbaric way in which the Nazi regime behaved has helped following generations to understand what was endured by so many. Extreme efforts were made by military leaders, politicians, judges and many others to ensure that Europe was able to rebuild and re-establish itself, and that justice was seen to be done wherever possible. No amount of compensation or, for that matter, "true" justice will ever compensate for the atrocities that were inflicted on innocent people during the war but, perhaps, through greater understanding, the world can ensure, collectively, that such events never occur again.

Terry Davis, the Chairman of the Council of Europe at the time of Simon Wiesenthal's death said by way of tribute: "Without Simon Wiesenthal's relentless effort to find Nazi criminals and bring them to justice and to fight anti-Semitism and prejudice, Europe would never have succeeded in healing its wounds and reconciling itself... He was a soldier of justice, which is indispensable to our freedom, stability and peace."

Many thousands of survivors of the Holocaust worldwide still bear the identification numbers tattooed on them when they were incarcerated by the Nazis. Every survivor lives with the unending, often unendurable, weight of the genocide which wiped out entire families and destroyed thousands of communities. Jewish populations the world over have never fully recovered from the inhumane blow they were dealt by Hitler and the Nazis. Many survivors suffer what is known as "survivor syndrome", experiencing acute anxiety, memory loss and other cognitive disorders, depression, withdrawal and guilt. Although Hitler was lionized during his heyday for his supposed military prowess and the inspirational leadership qualities he displayed in turning a nation which had been humbled by the Treaty of Versailles into a military superpower, for a while at least, he is undoubtedly remembered as a leader who brought suffering and death to millions. He cleverly groomed the SS and the *Wehrmacht* so that once they had grown inured to mass killings, through executing young Jewish males, the killing of women and children could be introduced to the Final Solution. Hitler and the Nazi Party rose to power skilfully and rapidly, but their fall was dramatic and equally precipitous. Despite the fact that the Second World War came to an end in 1945, the memory of the Holocaust has quite rightly been kept alive out of respect both for those who died and those who survived, and also to serve as a lesson which humanity should never forget.

Many of the concentration camps – such as Auschwitz pictured here – have been retained largely as they were as a permanent memorial to the millions who lost their lives during the Nazis' reign of terror.